# Citizenship
## Made Simple

An Easy-to-Read Guide to the
U.S. Citizenship Process

### 4th Edition

By Barbara Brooks Kimmel

and

Alan M. Lubiner, Esq.

Published by

## Next Decade
*books that simplify complex subjects*

Chester, New Jersey, USA
www.nextdecade.com

# *Citizenship Made Simple*
An Easy-to-Read Guide to the U.S. Citizenship Process

by Barbara Brooks Kimmel
and Alan M. Lubiner, Esq.

Published by:
**Next Decade, Inc.**
39 Old Farmstead Road
Chester, NJ 07930  USA
Telephone: (908) 879-6625
Fax: (908) 879-2920
E-mail: info@nextdecade.com

**Library of Congress Cataloging-in-Publication Data**

Kimmel, Barbara Brooks.
   Citizenship made simple : an easy-to-read guide to the U.S.
citizenship process / by Barbara Brooks Kimmel and Alan M. Lubiner.– 4th ed.
      p. cm.
Includes index.
   ISBN 1-932919-08-2
 1. Citizenship--United States. 2. Naturalization--United States.
I. Lubiner, Alan M. II. Title.
   KF4710.Z9K56 2006
   342.7308'3--dc22
   2005029026

$16.95 Soft cover

# Table of Contents _____

# About the Authors

Barbara Kimmel spent over fifteen years employed in the New York area as a relocation consultant to many international corporations and several prominent immigration lawyers. During that time she successfully guided thousands of aliens through the complex immigration process.

In 1990 Barbara began writing and publishing "books that simplify complex subjects". She has written four editions of **Citizenship Made Simple**, first published in 1996. Barbara is also the co-author of **Immigration Made Simple**, first published in 1990. These books have received outstanding professional reviews in *Library Journal* and *Booklist*, and have been Quality Books #1 bestsellers.

Finally, she is the President and Publisher at Next Decade, Inc. in Chester, New Jersey. Barbara's company was named Quality Book's **Publisher of the Year** at the 1997 Book Exposition in Chicago. For more information, visit our web site at www.nextdecade.com.

Ms. Kimmel was awarded a Bachelor of Arts Degree in International Affairs from Lafayette College in Pennsylvania and an MBA from the Bernard M. Baruch Graduate School of Business of the City University of New York.

❋ ❋ ❋

Alan Lubiner has been practicing Immigration Law since 1975. From 1975 until 1981, the Immigration & Naturalization Service employed him in a number of capacities including assisting in the drafting of legislation for the Select Commission on Immigration in Washington, DC. He also spent time in the United States Attorney's Office in the Southern District of Florida where he served as a Special Assistant United States Attorney assigned to special Immigration prosecutions.

In 1981, Mr. Lubiner opened a private law practice, with headquarters in Cranford, New Jersey and specializing in Immigration law. His practice is heavily concentrated in professionals, and he currently represents major corporations, individuals and universities in the scientific field with emphasis on computer science, electrical engineering, chemical engineering, chemistry and pharmaceutical research. He has successfully handled over 1000 cases for foreign students and other individuals.

Mr. Lubiner's credentials include a Bachelor of Science Degree in Finance from New York University and a Juris Doctorate degree from Brooklyn Law School. He is a member of the American Immigration Lawyers Association, an affiliated organization of the American Bar Association, and served on its Board of Governors. He is also a past Chairman of the New Jersey Chapter of the American Immigration Lawyer's Association, and a past chairman of the NJ State Bar Section on Immigration. Mr. Lubiner is a member of the Bar of the States of New Jersey, New York and Pennsylvania and is admitted to practice before the Federal Courts in New Jersey, New York and Pennsylvania, as well as the United States Supreme Court. Finally, he is the co-author of **Immigration Made Simple** and **Citizenship Made Simple**.

*With special thanks to all those who continue to recognize
the importance of our books*

✳ ✳ ✳

# *Disclaimer* _____

The purpose of this book is to provide interested individuals with a basic understanding of the rules and regulations concerning U.S. Citizenship procedures. It is sold with the understanding that the publisher and authors are not engaged in rendering legal or other professional services in this book, only in sharing information in regard to the subject matter covered.  If legal or other expert assistance is required, the services of a competent professional should be sought.

This manual was not written to provide all the information that is available to the authors/and or publisher on the subject of U.S. citizenship, but rather, to compliment, amplify and supplement other texts and available information. While every effort has been made to ensure that this book is as complete and accurate as possible, there may be mistakes, either typographical or in content.  Therefore, this text should be used as a general guide only, and not as the ultimate source of U.S. citizenship information. Furthermore, this book contains information on U.S. citizenship only up to the printing date. The rules and regulations change frequently.

The authors and Next Decade, Inc. shall not be held liable, nor be responsible to any person or entity with respect to any loss or damage caused, or alleged to be caused, directly or indirectly by the information contained in this book.

*If you do not wish to be bound by the above,*
*you may return this book to the publisher for a full refund.*

# *Introduction* _____

Over the past fifteen years we have been updating and publishing a book called **Immigration Made Simple, An Easy-to-Read Guide to the U.S. Immigration Process**. From our experience working with immigrants, we know that they all share one common characteristic. They lack knowledge of the U.S. Immigration process. So we have provided immigrants with reference material presented in simple language and laying out the basics of U.S. immigration regulations. There is an ongoing need, as rules change, and we continue to receive thousands of orders from every state in the U.S., and many foreign countries as well.

In 1996 we identified another need. More immigrants were applying for U.S. Citizenship then ever before. Again, they needed a reference guide that explained the basic rules and regulations, and so we published **Citizenship Made Simple**. This is the fourth edition. It was updated to reflect the changes in the processing of citizenship applications and to ensure timely information.

This book is an easy to use reference for foreign nationals who wish to apply for U.S. Citizenship. It can also be used by those who teach courses on U.S. Citizenship, English as a Second Language instructors, corporate personnel, educational institutions, business managers, legal support staff, and others who have occasion to work with our U.S. Immigration and Citizenship processes.

The order of the subject matter is intended to be useful. I start by defining some frequently used terms. The sections that follow describe the process of becoming a U.S. Citizen, the requirements, the application procedure, and the test. There is also information on U.S. history, important historical documents, the U.S. government, our holidays, and U.S. Presidents. A very important chapter including one hundred questions and answers to be used as a study guide for the U.S. Citizenship Exam follows this. We have added a two news chapters in this edition, one on Citizenship Base on Military Service and the other on Acquisition and Derivation of Citizenship. Finally, you will find sample forms, a Directory of Service Offices and U.S. Passport Agencies.

After you read the chapters that follow, we hope that you will have a better understanding of the process of applying for U.S. Citizenship, and that this book will serve as a helpful reference guide in the future.

**Barbara Brooks Kimmel**
**Alan M. Lubiner, Attorney**

# 1   *Definitions*

**Those applying for U.S. Citizenship will frequently see the following terms, and so it is best to know what they mean before reading this book.**

■ *Alien:* a person who is not a citizen or a national of the U.S. The term refers to all foreign nationals in the U.S., whether they are here temporarily or with permanent resident status. Although the term may seem strange to you, it is frequently used in the immigration field, and therefore in this book.

■ *Beneficiary:* an alien who is the recipient of an application filed on their behalf by another individual or organization.

■ *Citizen:* a person owing loyalty to and entitled by birth or naturalization to the protection of a state or nation.

■ *Citizenship:* having the status of a citizen, along with its rights, privileges and duties.

■ *Form N-400 Application for Naturalization:* the form that must be completed when applying for U.S. Citizenship. Other documents must accompany this form. *See Chapter 5.*

■ *Green Card:* a slang term for the identity document or alien registration receipt card issued to permanent resident (immigrant) aliens. The card includes the alien's photograph, fingerprint and signature. At one time the identity card was green, which is how it derived its name.

■ *Immigrant:* an alien who comes to the United States to live permanently.

■ *Naturalization:* a process by which permanent resident aliens can convert their status to U.S. citizenship. Naturalization permits the individual to obtain a U.S. passport and to vote in U.S. elections. Permanent residence and U.S. citizenship are not the same.

■ ***Oath of Allegiance:*** a formal declaration that must be made when one applies for U.S. Citizenship. *See Chapter 4.*

■ ***Passport:*** a document issued by a government that identifies the holder and his citizenship, and permits that individual to travel abroad.

■ ***Permanent Residence:*** the right to live permanently in the U.S. Individuals are given alien registration cards upon approval of their application for permanent residence and are thereafter called permanent resident aliens. Immigrant is another name for permanent resident alien.

■ ***United States:*** the geographical territory including the continental U.S., Alaska, Hawaii, Puerto Rico, Guam and the U.S. Virgin Islands.

■ ***US Citizenship & Immigration Services (USCIS):*** a branch of the Department of Homeland Security. The USCIS is responsible for processing all immigration and naturalization related applications made by, or on behalf of, foreign nationals. The USCIS maintains offices throughout the U.S. and in several foreign countries. The USCIS replaces the INS.

# 2 Reasons to Become a U.S. Citizen

**United States citizenship is desired by people all over the world. They want to become U.S. citizens for many reasons, the most common being:**

■ The right to vote: Only a U.S. citizen can vote in Federal, State and Local elections. This is usually viewed as the most important benefit of U.S. citizenship.

■ Employment: Certain jobs, including some with the Federal Government, have U.S. citizenship as a requirement for eligibility.

■ Travel with a U.S. passport: Only a U.S. citizen can travel with a U.S. passport. This right exempts the passport holder from having to apply for visas to enter many countries.

■ Sponsor family members: U.S. citizens may sponsor their spouse, parents, sons and daughters, and brothers and sisters.

■ Freedom from immigration scrutiny: A U.S. citizen cannot be deported.

■ Loyalty and a sense of belonging: A U.S. citizen can identify with the freedom guaranteed by the United States, a feeling which he or she may or may not have enjoyed elsewhere.

■ Reuniting Families: A U.S. citizen can sponsor other family members who may wish to join them in the U.S.

*Whatever your reasons,*
*the United States welcomes you.*

# 3 The Four Ways to Qualify for Citizenship

**There are four main ways to qualify to become citizen of the United States.**

**1. THROUGH BIRTH IN THE U.S. :**
Almost everyone born in the United States is a U.S. citizen.

**2. BY BIRTH OUTSIDE THE U.S. :**
To a parent or parents who are U.S. citizens. *See Chapter 9.*

***Note:*** *If either or both of your parents or grandparents were, or are, U.S. citizens, consult with an Immigration lawyer. The laws of citizenship are very complicated and have changed many times over the years. You may be a U.S. citizen, and not even know it!*

**3. AFTER YOUR BIRTH :**
By your parent or parents becoming U.S. citizens while you were still a child. *See Chapter 9.*

***Note:*** *Age restrictions apply, so check with an Immigration professional.*

**4. NATURALIZATION :**
The process of becoming a United States citizen that will be covered in this book.

# 4 *Requirements*

**In order to be eligible for naturalization you must:**

■ **Be eighteen years of age or older**

■ **Be a lawful permanent resident of the United States**
(have a green card)

■ **Be a permanent resident of the United States for five years**
If you obtained your green card through marriage to a United States citizen, you need only wait three years, instead of five.

There is an exception to the usual five-year residence requirement and the physical presence requirement for spouses of U.S. citizens who are U.S. government employees "regularly stationed abroad". In order to qualify, the applicant must be a lawful permanent resident of the U.S. and be married to a U.S. citizen. The U.S. citizen spouse must be regularly stationed abroad by one of the following:

1. The government of the United States including U.S. military personnel.

2. American institutions of research recognized by the Attorney General.

3. An American company engaged in the development of foreign trade and commerce in the U.S.

4. A public international organization in which the U.S. participates by treaty or statute.

5. A religious denomination having a bona fide organization in the U.S. (Priests, ministers or missionaries).

The spouse must have entered the US as a permanent resident. However, in these cases which fall under Section 319(b) of the Immigration & Nationality Act, the applicant does not need to show any prior residence or period of physical presence in the U.S. They must, however meet the three conditions below:

1. Come to the U.S. to be naturalized.

2. Must intend to join the U.S. citizen spouse at his or her employment outside the U.S. promptly after naturalization.

3. Must declare a good faith intention to take up residence within the U.S. immediately upon termination of the employment abroad of the U.S. citizen spouse.

The applicant must file the standard citizenship application as outlined in Chapter 5. However, arrangements should be made at the time of filing, with the USCIS office in which the applicant plans to take the test and oath of allegiance, for the case to be processed in accordance with USCIS guidelines for expeditious naturalization. Please note that although this seems like a simple and straightforward method for obtaining citizenship, these are not routine cases. It is best to retain the services of an immigration lawyer to assist you if you qualify.

■ **Have been physically present in the United States for at least one half of the required residency period**
(There are exceptions to this rule)

■ **Must not have been absent from the US for a continuous period of more than one year during the period for which continuous residence is required.** Absences for a continuous period of more than six months, but less than one year establish a rebuttable presumption of abandonment of residence.

■ **Must have resided continuously within the United States from the date the application for naturalization is filed up to the time of admission to citizenship.** Questions of abandonment are extremely complicated and if you have any extended absences you should consult an immigration professional.

■ **Reside in the State in which you apply for at least three months**

■ **Be a person of good moral character**

■ **Have the ability to speak, read and write English**
(there are exceptions to this rule)

■ **Have a basic knowledge of the history and government of the United States**

■ **Have no voluntary Communist affiliation**
(There are exceptions to this rule)

■ **Be willing to take this Oath of Allegiance to the United States:**

## OATH OF ALLEGIANCE

*I hereby declare, on oath, that I absolutely and entirely renounce and abjure all allegiance and fidelity to any foreign prince, potentate, state or sovereignty of whom or which I have heretofore been a subject or citizen; that I will support and defend the Constitution and laws of the United States of America against all enemies, foreign and domestic; that I will bear true faith and allegiance to the same; \* that I will bear arms on behalf of the United States when required by law; \* that I will perform noncombatant service in the Armed Forces of the United States when required by law; that I will perform work of national importance under civilian direction when required by law; and that I take this obligation freely without any mental reservation or purpose of evasion; so help me God.*

\* In some cases, the USCIS will allow these clauses to be omitted.

# 5 *How to Apply*_____

**The application for citizenship consists of the following documents:**

- **Your cover letter**
- **Form N-400 Application for Naturalization**
- **Biometrics fee of $70.00 payable to USCIS**
- **Photographs**
- **Copy of front and back of your green card**
- **Filing fee of $320.00 payable to USCIS**

You can file your Application for Naturalization up to three months in advance of your actual eligibility date.

You must first obtain a Form N-400 from the USCIS. You can request the forms by calling **1-800-870 FORMS**. You may also download forms from the USCIS web site at http://uscis.gov/graphics/forms/fee/forms/index.htm.

Form N-400 must be completed with all the requested information. Do not leave blanks or the USCIS may send the application back, thereby delaying the process.

Your fingerprints will be taken at a future date by the USCIS. This is why you must send a separate check for $70.00 when you file your application. The USCIS will send you a receipt and will schedule you for an appointment to have your fingerprints taken at a USCIS facility near your residence.

You will also need two color passport style photographs. Write your name and alien registration number (green card number starting with "Λ") on the back of your pictures with a felt tipped pen. Do not staple or bend the pictures.

Assemble your completed cover letter, Form N-400, check for $70.00 for biometrics, the two photographs, and a copy of the front and back of your green card, together with a check for $320.00. Send this package by certified mail to the USCIS

Regional Service Center that has jurisdiction over your place of residence. (Certified mail is not required, but it is recommended so that you have proof of mailing). A list of the USCIS Regional Service Centers and the areas they serve can be found in Chapter 18. **Make sure to keep a photocopy of your completed application for your records.**

You will receive an appointment in the mail to take your citizenship test. Your interview and test will be conducted at your local USCIS District Office.

# 6 *Child Citizenship Act of 2000*

**This Act took effect on February 27, 2001 to automatically confer citizenship upon certain children born abroad who did not acquire U.S. citizenship at birth.**

The requirements for automatic citizenship are:

- At least one parent of the child must be a U.S. citizen, either by birth or naturalization

- The child is under the age of 18

- The child is residing in the U.S. with a green card, and is in the legal and physical custody of the U.S. citizen parent

- If the child is adopted, the adoption has been finalized

It does not matter in which order the above requirements are met, citizenship is acquired automatically as soon as all of the requirements have been met.

Children who reside abroad, that is, do not enter the U.S. with green cards, and who do not become U.S. citizens at birth, can also become citizens under this new law, however, they must apply to the USCIS for a certificate of citizenship. The requirements are:

- At least one parent of the child is a U.S. citizen, either by birth or through naturalization

- The U.S. citizen parent must have been physically present in the U.S. for a total of at least 5 years, at least 2 of which were after the age of 14. If the child's U.S. citizen parent does not meet this requirement, it is enough if one of the child's U.S. citizen parent's have a U.S. citizen parent that can meet it. (child's U.S. citizen grandparent).

■   The child is under the age of 18.

■   The child resides abroad in the legal and physical custody of the U.S. citizen parent and has been lawfully admitted into the U.S. as a nonimmigrant.

# 7 Citizenship Based on Military Service

**Since 1862, the naturalization laws have provided special benefits for aliens who served honorably in the U.S. armed forces.**

There are two basic provisions of law allowing the naturalization of those who have served in the military. Most recently, the laws also have provided a streamlined process for those military personnel serving on active duty status or recently discharged. In addition, for the first time, a serviceman/servicewoman who dies in combat or as a result of combat may receive posthumous citizenship.

Normally the law requires a person to have been a lawful permanent resident for five years before being eligible for naturalization. This time period is waived for servicemen/servicewomen who have served honorably on active duty for at least one year. The key word is "honorably". One who has received an undesirable or dishonorable discharge does not qualify. In addition, one who has procured relief or discharge from military service on the ground that he is a noncitizen is expressly disqualified from becoming a U.S. citizen except under special circumstances.

The naturalization application must be filed while the petitioner is still in the service or within six months after termination. A person who applies for naturalization under this section of law must comply with all requirements of the naturalization laws, both substantive and procedural, with the following exceptions:

- The application can be filed in any USCIS Office, regardless of the applicant's place of residence.

- No fees will be charged when you file for naturalization.

- The naturalization process will be made available overseas to members of the Armed Forces at U.S. embassies, consulates, and where practical, military installations.

Those with Acitve-Duty U.S. Military Service during specified periods of hostilities may also be naturalized without regard to periods of residence in the U.S. Those periods include:

— World War I, defined by regulation as beginning April 6, 1917 and ending November 11, 1918.

— World War II, for this purpose specified in the statute as beginning September 1, 1939 and ending December 31, 1946.

— The Korean hostilities, for this purpose specified in the statute as beginning June 25, 1950 and ending July 1, 1955.

— The Vietnam hostilities, specified in the statute as beginning February 28, 1961 and ending on a termination date to be fixed by Executive Order. An Executive Order terminated the Vietnam hostilities for this purpose on October 15, 1978.

— During any subsequent period of hostilities designated as such by Executive Order.

— A 1994 Executive Order authorized expedited naturalization for noncitizens who served honorably in active-duty status between August 2, 1990 and April 11, 1991 in the Persian Gulf conflict. This time period covers both "Operation Desert Shield" and "Operation Desert Storm."

— A July 3, 2002 Executive Order authorized expedited naturalization for noncitizens who served in an active-duty status in the "war against terrorists of global reach." The order designated September 11, 2001 as the start date for this designated armed conflict. A terminating date will be set by a future Executive Order.

On October 1, 1991, the President signed the Armed Forces Immigration Adjustment Act granting special immigrant status to noncitizens who have served honorably or are enlisted to serve in the military for at least 12 years. The Act benefits primarily about 3,000 Filipino sailors in the U.S. Navy.

## EXEMPTIONS

A person who applies for naturalization under this section of law must comply with all requirements of the naturalization laws, both substantive and procedural, with the following modifications:

■ He or she may be naturalized regardless of age.

■ The preclusion of naturalization because of an outstanding deportation proceeding or order does not apply.

■ The special restrictions relating to alien enemies do not apply.

■ The generally prescribed requirements of five years residence and requisite physical presence in the United States, and three months residence in a state or USCIS district, do not apply.

No residence in the jurisdiction of the USCIS district is required, and the petition can be filed in any Service district, regardless of petitioner's place of residence.

The regulations require good moral character as well as an attachment to the principles of the Constitution for one year before the naturalization application.

**Forms you will need to complete and submit:**

> ■ **N-400, Application for Naturalization**
>
> ■ **N-426, Request for Certification of Military or Naval Service** (This form requires certification by the military prior to submission to USCIS)
>
> ■ **G-325B, Biographic Information**

**Forms and Handbooks**
To get these forms, you can call the USCIS Form Line at: **1-800-870-3676** to request the "Military Packet".

# 8 *Dual Citizenship*

**Some countries generally allow individuals to carry dual citizenship with the U.S. while other countries do not. If you are concerned about losing your current citizenship when you become a naturalized U.S. citizen, you should speak to a representative of your government before filing for naturalization.**

You will find two lists below. The first is a list of countries that generally allow dual citizenship after naturalization. The second is a list of countries that generally do not allow dual citizenship after naturalization.

## DUAL CITIZENSHIP GENERALLY ALLOWED
## AFTER U.S. NATURALIZATION

Argentina, Australia, Barbados, Belize, Benin, Brazil, Bulgaria, Burkina FASO, Cambodia, Canada, Cape Verde, Central African Republic, Colombia, Costa Rica, Cote d'Ivoire, Croatia, Cyprus, Dominica, Dominican Republic, Ecuador, El Salvador, France, Ghana, Greece, Grenada, Guatemala, Hong Kong, Hungary, Iran, Ireland, Israel, Jamaica, Latvia, Lesotho, Liechtenstein, Macao, Maldives, Malta, Mexico, Morocco, Nevis, New Zealand, Nigeria, Namibia, Panama, Peru, Poland, Portugal, Romania, Russia, St. Christopher, St. Kitts, St. Lucia, Slovenia, Sri Lanka, Switzerland, Syria, Togo, Tunisia, Turkey, Tuvalu, United Kingdom, Uruguay.

## DUAL CITIZENSHIP GENERALLY NOT ALLOWED
## AFTER U.S. NATURALIZATION

Algeria, Andorra, Austria, Azerbaijan, Bahrain, Belarus, Belgium, Bhutan, Bolivia, Botswana, Brunei, Buruni, Cameroon, Congo, Chile, China, Cuba, Czech Republic, Denmark, Djibouti, Equatorial Guinea, Estonia *after 1992*, Finland, Gabon, Guinea,

Honduras, Iceland, India, Indonesia, Iraq, Italy, Japan, Kaakhstan, Kiribati, Korea, Kuwait, Kyrgyz Republic, Laos, Libya, Luxembourg, Malawi, Malaysia, Mali, Mexico, Monaco, Myanmar/ (Burma), Nepal, Netherlands, New Guinea, Nicaragua, Niger, North Korea, Norway, Oman, Pakistan, Palau, Papua New Guinea, Philippines, Principe Island, Quatar, Rwanda, Saudi Arabia, Sierra Leone, Singapore, Slovac Republic, South Africa (with exceptions), South Korea, Spain, Sudan, Swaziland, Sweden, Taiwan, Tonga, Uganda, Ukraine, United Arab Emirates, Uzbekistan, Venezuela, Vietnam, Yemen, Zimbabwe.

# 9 Acquisition and Derivation of Citizenship

## ACQUISITION OF CITIZENSHIP AT BIRTH

We all know that a child born in the United States is a citizen at birth, but a child born outside of the United States may also acquire United States citizenship at birth under certain circumstances. Following are some of the current rules:

- A child born outside of the United States to two U.S. citizen parents generally acquires U.S. citizenship at birth.

- A child born outside of the U.S. to one citizen parent may also acquire U.S. citizenship at birth under certain circumstances, depending upon the date of the child's birth. For example, a child born outside of the U.S. after November 14, 1986, may become a U.S. citizen at birth if his U.S. citizen parent was physically present in the U.S. five years prior to the child's birth, two of those years being after age 14. If the child was born between December 24, 1952 and November 14, 1986, the U.S. citizen parent must have been physically present in the U.S. for ten years prior to the child's birth, five of those years being after age 14.

There are exceptions to these rules and different laws for children born prior to December 24, 1952. The laws covering this have changed numerous times over the years and it is beyond the scope of this book to cover every scenario. We strongly recommend that you consult an experienced immigration practitioner if you feel you may have a claim to U.S. citizenship at birth.

## DERIVATION OF CITIZENSHIP AFTER BIRTH

A child may also become a U.S. citizen after birth, depending upon the status of his or her parent or parents.

The Child Citizenship Act of 2000 is covered in Chapter 6, but a child may also become a US citizen under the laws in effect prior to February 27, 2001, the effective date of the Child Citizenship Act of 2000.

Children born after December 24, 1952 but before February 27, 2001, who were lawfully admitted to the United States for permanent residence become U.S. citizens automatically upon the naturalization of both of their parents, their surviving parent or the parent having legal custody (or upon the naturalization of one parent if the other was a citizen at birth).

As with acquisition of citizenship at birth, the laws covering this have changed many times over the years and we cannot cover all of the scenarios in this book. Again we highly recommend that you seek the counsel of an experienced immigration practitioner if you think you may have a claim to U.S. citizenship.

# 10 The Test

**In order to become a United States citizen, you must first prove that you can read, write and speak English, and that you have a basic understanding of the history and government of the United States.**

*Note: Some people are exempt from the English requirement because of age and long residence in the U.S, or because of a medically certified physical disability. If you have been a permanent resident of the United States for at least fifteen years or you have a physical disability; consult with an Immigration Lawyer to see if you might qualify for an exemption.*

When you are called for an interview at the USCIS, the Immigration Examiner will speak to you in English. He or she will ask you all the questions that are contained on the Form N-400 that you completed. You must show that you understand what the Examiner is asking, and you must answer the questions in English.

You will be asked to write at least one sentence in English and possibly more if the Examiner has doubts about your ability to write in English. There are no standard sentences. The Examiner will use his or her discretion in determining what to ask, basing their decision on your level of education and background.

You will also be tested on your understanding of the history and government of the United States. The USCIS Examiner does not expect you to have the knowledge of a college professor, but you are expected to understand our system of government and how it works, how and why our country was founded, and important events in the history of the United States.

The questions you will be asked will usually be taken from the list found in Chapter 16. If you study and learn the questions and answers on that list, you should easily pass the test.

The U.S. Government publishes free study guides, and your Public Library may also have study materials. Ask you librarian for help in finding a book that will aid you in preparing for the U.S. Citizenship test. You can also enroll in a study course given by your local High School or Community College Adult Education Department.

Enrollment in such a course is highly recommended for those who do not feel certain about their ability to pass the U.S. Citizenship test.

The application must be approved or denied within four months of the interview. Assuming it is approved, the final swearing-in ceremony will be held the same day, or at a later date, depending on the current procedure at your local USCIS office. At the time of the swearing-in ceremony, the applicant is required to take the Oath of Allegiance to the United States of America (*see complete text in Chapter 4*), and sign this oath.

You will then be given a Certificate of Naturalization. With this document, you can obtain a U.S. Passport. *See Chapter 19 for addresses of U.S. Passport Offices.*

# 11 A Brief History of the United States

The first Europeans to reach North America were Icelandic Vikings led by Leif Ericson in about the year 1000, but they did not establish a settlement.

According to popular history, the United States was discovered in 1492 by Christopher Columbus, an Italian navigator, in service to the King and Queen of Spain. They were interested in creating a shorter route between the East and the West to facilitate the purchase of Asian dyes, spices and textiles. America actually got its name from another Italian navigator named Amerigo Vespucci.

Explorers from England, France and Spain were all trying to claim territory for their homeland. The English claimed the Northeast where the original thirteen colonies were established. The Spanish claimed Florida and surrounding areas, and the French took the land around the Mississippi River.

The first English colony was founded in Jamestown, Virginia in 1607. A few years later, English Puritans came to America to escape religious persecution for their opposition to the Church of England. These Pilgrims sailed to America on the Mayflower and founded the colony of Plymouth in New England in 1620. This early colony later became Massachusetts. The American Indians helped the Pilgrims to adjust to their new life in America. Interestingly, the Puritans practiced a form of intolerant moralism and in 1636 an English clergyman named Roger Williams left Massachusetts and founded the colony of Rhode Island to guarantee religious freedom and separation of Church and State.

By 1733, the original thirteen colonies had been established along the Atlantic Coast. These colonies became the first states: Connecticut, Delaware, Georgia, Maryland, Massachusetts, New Hampshire, New Jersey, New York, North Carolina, Pennsylvania, Rhode Island, South Carolina, and Virginia.

During the eighteenth century, America was the host to several wars fought primarily between the French and the English for control of land. The French finally lost and ceded all the land east of the Mississippi River to England.

In the middle 1770's the First Continental Congress met in Philadelphia. It was made up of representatives from all the colonies that were generally upset with their lack of independence from England, their mother country. The following year the Second Continental Congress met and Thomas Jefferson wrote the Declaration of Independence. The colonies essentially declared their freedom from England.

When the King and Queen of England learned of this, the Revolutionary War (American Revolution) ensued between England and the colonists, lead by George Washington. On July 4, 1776 the colonies declared their freedom and independence from England and the United States was born, even though the Revolutionary War did not officially end until 1783 with the Treaty of Paris, by which England recognized American independence. The turning point in the war came in 1777 when American soldiers defeated the British Army at Saratoga, New York. One of our famous American Revolutionary leaders was Patrick Henry, who is best known for his slogan "Give me liberty or give me death."

The new Americans wrote the Constitution to alleviate their fear of excessive central power, and appointed their first President, George Washington, in 1789. The United States of America grew and flourished as land was purchased from the French and Spanish. The largest land acquisition was The Louisiana Purchase in 1803 that almost doubled the size of the U.S.

Land didn't always come easy to the new Americans. The Mexican War was fought against Mexico from 1846-1848 for control of the land now known as Texas. As part of winning the War, the Americans also gained control of land now comprising the States of Arizona, California, Colorado, New Mexico and Nevada. The Americans later fought with Spain in the Spanish American War, winning the U.S. territories of Guam, the U.S. Virgin Islands and the Philippines.

The Civil War, between the Northern and Southern states, was fought from 1861-1865 when Abraham Lincoln was President. It is considered by many to have been the most traumatic episode in American history. The Northern states won the war and slavery was abolished. This war also put an end to the idea that the country was a collection of semi-independent states and the U.S. became an indivisible whole.

After the Civil War, the U.S. became a leading industrial power and the first transcontinental railroad was completed in 1869. This brought about the rise of organized labor and the American Federation of Labor was founded in 1886. The late 19th century was also a period of enormous immigration into the U.S.

The United States fought in World War I (1914-1918), siding with England and France against Germany. Woodrow Wilson was President. After the War, the United

States turned inward and withdrew from affairs in Europe. Congress enacted immigration restrictions in 1921 and further tightened them in 1924 and 1929.

The 1920's were golden years as the U.S. became a consumer society. But with profits soaring, people began to speculate in the Stock Market. In 1929, the bubble burst with the Stock Market crash and America was sent into the Great Depression. Thousands of banks and over 100,000 businesses failed. One out of every four workers was unemployed. In 1932 Franklin D. Roosevelt was elected President on "a New Deal for the American people". Although the economy improved, full recovery did not come until World War II.

The United States tried to remain neutral when war broke out in Europe in 1939. But when the Pearl Harbor Naval Base was bombed by the Japanese in December 1941, the U.S. entered the war, first against Japan, and then against its allies, Germany and Italy. The United States was allied with many countries including Britain, France, the old USSR, Australia and Canada. World War II lasted until 1945 when President Harry Truman ordered the use of atomic bombs in the Japanese cities of Hiroshima and Nagaski. Nearly 200,000 civilians were killed.

After the end of the war, The United Nations was formed, a type of "international congress". Soon tensions rose between the U.S. and its ally, the Soviet Union as Joseph Stalin imposed Communist dictatorships in eastern Europe. This became known as the "Cold War". The Korean War also arose as a result of Stalin's actions. Armed with Soviet weapons, North Korea invaded South Korea. The war lasted for three hears (1950-1953) and left Korea divided. But, tensions between the Soviet Union and the United States continued to grow as the Soviets developed atomic and hydrogen bombs.

The period between 1945 and 1970 was one of economic growth for the United States. In 1960 John F. Kennedy was elected President. In 1962 President Kennedy faced a dramatic crisis in the Cold War. The Soviet Union was caught installing nuclear missiles in Cuba, close enough to threaten major American cities. Kennedy imposed a naval blockade on the island of Cuba and the Soviets agreed to remove the missiles. Kennedy's assassination in 1963 was a terrible blow for the American people.

Lyndon B. Johnson was John F. Kennedy's successor as President. Although his "War on Poverty" established many beneficial social programs for the poor and undereducated, he also became preoccupied with the Vietnam War in the late 1960's. Although many viewed this war as a continued effort to check Communism, many others felt that Americans had no business in Vietnam and anti-war demonstrations broke out across the U.S. Richard Nixon was elected President in 1968 and by 1973 a peace treaty was signed with North Vietnam.

Richard Nixon is credited with reestablishing relations with the People's Republic of China and negotiating the first Strategic Arms Limitation Treaty with the Soviet Union. Although he easily won reelection in 1972, he was soon implicated in a reelection coverup that became known as Watergate. When it became clear that he was going to be impeached by Congress and convicted, he became the first, and only, U.S. president to resign from office.

As the century drew to a close, a string of twenty six years of Democratic control was broken in 1980 when Republicans gained a majority seat in the U.S. Senate and Ronald Reagan was elected president. American voting patterns have remained volatile since then. In 1983 the U.S. economy entered into one of its longest periods of sustained growth in American history. Although the economy remains strong, many Americans perceive a decline in the strength of the family and the general quality of life.

On September 11, 2001, our country became the victim of one of the worst terrorist attacks in history. In fact, a new chapter in the lives of Americans opened that day as we learn to adjust and adapt to a world of tightened security and zero tolerance for terrorism. The United States remains the strongest nation in the world. We continue to welcome immigrants with the hope that one day each immigrant will choose to become a U.S. citizen.

# 12 *Important Documents in Our Nation's History_*

**Some of the more important documents in the history of the United States are:**

**The Mayflower Compact**

In November 1620 each male adult who had sailed on the Mayflower from Plymouth England bound for Virginia, signed the Mayflower Compact in Cape Cod Harbor. It was the first colonial agreement that formed a "government by consent of the governed" and gave the settlers the power to develop and enact laws for the good of the settlement. This group of Pilgrims was led by William Bradford.

**The Declaration of Independence**

This document declared our freedom from England in 1776, and was formally adopted on July 4, 1776. It was originally written by Thomas Jefferson and signed by the Representatives from the original thirteen colonies (New York being the last), thus beginning our great nation. The basic belief of the Declaration of Independence is "that all men are created equal". The original colonies (the first states) were Connecticut, Delaware, Georgia, Maryland, Massachusetts, New Hampshire, New Jersey, New York, North Carolina, Pennsylvania, Rhode Island, South Carolina, and Virginia.

*The entire text of the Declaration of Independence is reproduced at the end of this chapter.*

## The Articles of Confederation

This was the first Constitution of the United States, adopted in 1781 by the original thirteen states. It remained in effect until 1788 when the present Constitution was ratified. The articles created a loose confederation of independent states and gave limited power to the central government.

## The Constitution

The Constitution is the "Supreme law of the land". It protects the rights of everyone living in the United States (citizens and non-citizens alike). Delegates of twelve of the original thirteen states met in Philadelphia at the Constitutional Convention in May 1787 to revise the Articles of Confederation. Rhode Island failed to send a representative as they were afraid of national regulation. George Washington led the session, which lasted until September. It went into effect on the first Wednesday in March 1789, with New Hampshire casting the ninth vote needed for a two-thirds majority approval on June 21, 1788. The original Constitution had a Preamble (introduction), and seven parts or Articles.

### The Preamble read as follows:

*We the people of the United States, in order to form a more perfect Union, establish Justice, insure domestic tranquillity, provide for the common defense, promote the general welfare, and secure the blessings of liberty to ourselves and our posterity, do ordain and establish this Constitution for the United States of America.*

### The original seven Articles dealt with the following issues:

1. Establishing the Legislative Branch to make the laws
2. Establishing the Executive Branch to enforce the laws
3. Establishing the Judicial Branch to interpret the laws
4. What powers should be given to the States
5. Adding or making changes to the Constitution
6. Handling debts and treaties
7. How many State votes would be necessary to accept the Constitution.

The Constitution can only be changed by an amendment. The first ten amendments to the Constitution were ratified on December 15, 1791 and were named the Bill of Rights. There have been a total of twenty- six amendments since that time.

***The entire text of the original Constitution is reproduced at the end of this chapter.***

**Bill of Rights**

**The first ten amendments to the Constitution submitted by Congress in 1790 and adopted in 1791 were:**

| | |
|---|---|
| **Article I** | Freedom of religion, speech, of the press, and right of petition. |
| **Article II** | Right of the people to bear arms not to be infringed. |
| **Article III** | Quartering of troops. |
| **Article IV** | Persons and houses to be secure from unreasonable searches and seizures. |
| **Article V** | Trials for crimes; just compensation for private property taken for public use. |
| **Article VI** | Civil rights in trials for crimes enumerated. |
| **Article VII** | Civil rights in civil suits. |
| **Article VIII** | Excessive bail, fines, and punishments prohibited. |
| **Article IX** | Reserved rights of people. |
| **Article X** | Powers not delegated, reserved to states and people respectively. |

**The Monroe Doctrine**

This was written by President James Monroe and announced during his message to Congress on December 2, 1823. Basically, it established a policy of opposing interference by other countries, in the affairs of the United States. It was originally developed out of concern by the U.S. and Great Britain of European colonial expansion in the Americas.

# Text of the Declaration of Independence

## In Congress July 4, 1776, The Unanimous Declaration of The Thirteen United States of America

When in the Course of human events, it becomes necessary for one people to dissolve the political bands which have connected them with another, and to assume among the Powers of the earth, the separate and equal station to which the Laws of Nature and of Nature's God entitle them, a decent respect to the opinions of mankind requires that they should declare the causes which impel them to the separation.

We hold these truths to be self-evident, that all men are created equal, that they are endowed by their Creator with certain unalienable Rights, that among these are Life, Liberty, and the pursuit of Happiness. That to secure these rights, Governments are instituted among Men, deriving their just powers from the consent of the governed. That whenever any Form of Government becomes destructive of these ends, it is the Right of the People to alter or to abolish it, and to institute new Government, having its foundation on such principles and organizing its powers in such form, as to them shall seem most likely to effect their Safety and Happiness. Prudence, indeed, will dictate that Governments long established should not be changed for light and transient causes; and accordingly all experience hath shown that mankind are more disposed to suffer, while evils are sufferable, than to right themselves by abolishing the forms to which they are accustomed. But when a long train of abuses and usurpations pursuing invariably the same Object evinces a design to reduce them under absolute Despotism, it is their right, it is their duty, to throw off such Government, and to provide new Guards for their future security. Such has been the patient suffrance of these Colonies; and such is now the necessity which constrains them to alter their former Systems of Government. The history of the present King of Great Britain is a history of repeated injuries and usurpations, all having in direct object the establishment of an absolute Tyranny over these States. To prove this, let Facts be submitted to a candid world.

He has refused his Assent to Laws, the most wholesome and necessary for the public good.

He has forbidden his Governors to pass laws of immediate and pressing importance, unless suspended in their operation till his Assent should be obtained; and when so suspended, has utterly neglected to attend to them.

He has refused to pass other Laws for the accommodation of large districts of people, unless those people would relinquish the right of Representation in the Legislature, a right inestimable to them and formidable to tyrants only.

He has called together legislative bodies at places unusual, uncomfortable, and distant from the depository of their Public Records, for the sole purpose of fatiguing them into compliance with his measures.

He has dissolved Representative Houses repeatedly, for opposing with manly firmness his invasions on the rights of the people.

He has refused for a long time, after such dissolutions, to cause others to be elected; whereby the Legislative Powers, incapable of Annihilation, have returned to the People at large for their exercise; the State remaining in the meantime exposed to all the dangers of invasion from without, and convulsions within.

He has endeavored to prevent the population of these States; for that purpose obstructing the Laws for Naturalization of Foreigners; refusing to pass others to encourage their migration hither, and raising the conditions of new Appropriations of Lands.

He has obstructed the Administration of Justice, by refusing his Assent to Laws for establishing Judiciary Powers.

He has made Judges dependent on his Will alone, for the tenure of their offices, and the amount and payment of their salaries.

He has erected a multitude of New Offices, and sent hither swarms of Officers to harass our people, and eat out their substance.

He has kept among us, in times of peace, Standing Armies without the Consent of our legislatures.

He has affected to render the military independent of and superior to the Civil Power.

He has combined with others to subject us to a jurisdiction foreign to our constitution, and unacknowledged by our laws; giving his Assent to their acts of pretended legislation.

For quartering large bodies of armed troops among us:

For protecting them, by a mock Trial, from Punishment for any Murders which they should commit on the Inhabitants of these States:

For cutting off our Trade with all parts of the world:

For imposing taxes on us without our Consent:

For depriving us in many cases, of the benefits of Trial by Jury:

For transporting us beyond Seas to be tried for pretended offenses:

For abolishing the free System of English Laws in a neighboring Province, establishing therein an Arbitrary government, and enlarging its Boundaries so as to render it at once an example and fit instrument for introducing the same absolute rule into these Colonies:

For taking away our Charters, abolishing our most valuable Laws, and altering fundamentally, the Forms of our Governments:

For suspending our own Legislatures, and declaring themselves invested with Power to legislate for us in all cases whatsoever:

He has abdicated Government here, by declaring us out of his Protection and waging War against us.

He has plundered our seas, ravaged our Coasts, burnt our towns, and destroyed the lives of our people.

He is at this time transporting large armies of foreign mercenaries to compleat the works of death, desolation and tyranny, already begun with circumstances of Cruelty & perfidy scarcely paralleled in the most barbarous ages, and totally unworthy the Head of a civilized nation.

He has constrained our fellow Citizen taken Captive on the high Seas to bear Arms against their Country, to become the executioners of their friends and Brethren, or to fall themselves by their Hands.

He has excited domestic insurrections amongst us, and has endeavored to bring on the inhabitants of our frontiers, the merciless Indian Savages, whose known rule of warfare, is an undistinguished destruction of all ages, sexes and conditions.

In every stage of these Oppressions We have Petitioned for Redress in the most humble terms: Our repeated Petitions have been answered only by repeated injury. A Prince, whose character is thus marked by every act which may define a Tyrant, is unfit to be the ruler of a free people.

Nor have We been wanting in attention to our British brethren. We have warned them from time to time of attempts by their legislature to extend an unwarrantable jurisdiction over us. We have reminded them of the circumstances of our emigration and settlement here. We have appealed to their native justice and magnanimity, and we have conjured them by the ties of our common kindred to disavow these usurpations, which would inevitably interrupt our connection and correspondence. They too have been deaf to the voice of justice and of consanguinity. We must, therefore, acquiesce in the necessity, which denounces our Separation, and hold them, as we hold the rest of mankind, Enemies in War, in Peace Friends.

We, therefore, the Representatives of the United States of America, in General Congress, assembled, appealing to the Supreme Judge of the world for the rectitude of our intentions, do, in the name, and by authority of the good People of these Colonies, solemnly publish and declare, That these United Colonies are, and of Right ought to be Free and Independent States; that they are Absolved from all Allegiance to the British Crown, and that all political connection between them and the State of Great Britain, is and ought to be totally dissolved; and that as Free and Independent States, they have full power to levy War, conclude Peace, contract Alliances, establish Commerce, and to do all other Acts and Things which Independent States may of right do. And for the support of this Declaration, with a firm reliance on the Protection of Divine Providence, we mutually pledge to each other our Lives, our Fortunes and our sacred Honor.

# *Text of the Constitution*

## Preamble
*We the People of the United States, in Order to form a more perfect Union, establish Justice, insure domestic Tranquility, provide for the common defence, promote the general Welfare, and secure the Blessings of Liberty to ourselves and our Posterity, do ordain and establish this Constitution for the United States of America.*

## Article I
*Section 1.* All legislative Powers herein granted shall be vested in a Congress of the United States, which shall consist of a Senate and House of Representatives.

*Section 2.* The House of Representatives shall be composed of Members chosen every second Year by the People of the several States, and the Electors in each State shall have the Qualifications requisite for Electors of the most numerous Branch of the State Legislature.

No Person shall be a Representative who shall not have attained to the Age of twenty five Years, and been seven Years a Citizen of the United States, and who shall not, when elected, be an Inhabitant of that State in which he shall be chosen.

Representatives and direct Taxes shall be apportioned among the several States which may be included within this Union, according to their respective Numbers, which shall be determined by adding to the whole Number of free Persons, including those bound to Service for a Term of Years, and excluding Indians not taxed, three fifths of all other Persons. The actual Enumeration shall be made within three Years after the first Meeting of the Congress of the United States, and within every subsequent Term of ten Years, in such Manner as they shall by Law direct. The Number of Representatives shall not exceed one for every thirty Thousand, but each State shall have at Least one Representative; and until such enumeration shall be made, the State of New Hampshire shall be entitled to choose three, Massachusetts eight, Rhode Island and Providence Plantations one, Connecticut five, New York six, New Jersey four, Pennsylvania eight, Delaware one, Maryland six, Virginia ten, North Carolina five, South Carolina five, and Georgia three.

When vacancies happen in the Representation from any State, the Executive Authority thereof shall issue Writs of Election to fill such Vacancies.

The House of Representatives shall choose their speaker and other Officers; and shall have the sole Power of Impeachment.

*Section 3.* The Senate of the United States shall be composed of two Senators from each State, chosen by the Legislature thereof, for six Years; and each Senator shall have one Vote.

Immediately after they shall be assembled in Consequence of the first Election, they shall be divided as equally as may be into three Classes. The Seats of the Senators of the first Class shall be vacated at the Expiration of the second Year, of the second Class at the Expiration of the fourth Year, and of the third Class at the Expiration of the sixth Year, so that one third may be chosen every second Year; and if Vacancies happen by Resignation, or otherwise, during the Recess of the Legislature of any State, the Executive thereof may make temporary Appointments until the next Meeting of the Legislature, which shall then fill such Vacancies.

No Person shall be a Senator who shall not have attained to the Age of thirty Years, and been nine Years a citizen of the United States, and who shall not, when elected, be an Inhabitant of that State for which he shall be chosen.

The Vice President of the United States shall be President of the Senate, but shall have no Vote, unless they be equally divided.

The Senate shall choose their other Officers, and also a President pro tempore, in the Absence of the Vice President, or when he shall exercise the Office of President of the United States.

The Senate shall have the sole Power to try all Impeachments. When sitting for that Purpose, they shall be on Oath or Affirmation. When the President of the United States is tried, the Chief Justice shall preside: And no Person shall be convicted without the Concurrence of two thirds of the Members present.

Judgment in Cases of Impeachment shall not extend further than to removal from Office, and disqualification to hold and enjoy any Office of honor, Trust or Profit under the United States: but the Party convicted shall nevertheless be liable and subject to Indictment, Trial, Judgment and Punishment, according to law.

*Section 4.* The Times, Places, and Manner of holding Elections for Senators and Representatives, shall be prescribed in each State by the Legislature thereof; but the Congress may at any time by Law make or alter such Regulations, except as to the Places of choosing Senators.

The Congress shall assemble at least once in every Year, and such Meeting shall be on the first Monday in December, unless they shall by Law appoint a different Day.

*Section 5.* Each House shall be the Judge of the Elections, Returns, and Qualifications of its own Members, and a Majority of each shall constitute a Quorum to do Business; but a smaller Number may adjourn from day to day, and may be authorized to compel the Attendance of absent Members, in such Manner, and under such Penalties as each House may provide.

Each House may determine the Rules of its Proceedings, punish its Members for disorderly Behaviour, and, with the Concurrence of two thirds, expel a Member.

Each House shall keep a journal of its Proceedings, and from time to time publish the same, excepting such Parts as may in their Judgment require Secrecy; and the Yeas and Nays of the Members of either House on any question shall, at the Desire of one fifth of those Present, be entered on the journal.

Neither House, during the Session of Congress, shall, without the Consent of the other, adjourn for more than three days, nor to any other Place than that in which the two Houses shall be sitting.

*Section 6.* The Senators and Representatives shall receive a Compensation for their Services, to be ascertained by Law, and paid out of the Treasury of the United States. They shall in all Cases, except Treason, Felony and Breach of the Peace, be privileged from Arrest during their Attendance at the Session of their respective Houses, and in going to and returning from the same; and for any Speech or Debate in either House, they shall not be questioned in any other Place.

No Senator or Representative shall, during the Time for which he was elected, be appointed to any civil Office under the Authority of the United States, which shall have been created, or the Emoluments whereof shall have been increased during such time; and no Person holding any Office under the United States, shall be a Member of either House during his Continuance in Office.

*Section 7.* All Bills for raising Revenue shall originate in the House of Representatives; but the Senate may propose or concur with Amendments as on other Bills.

Every Bill which shall have passed the House of Representatives and the Senate, shall, before it become a Law, be presented to the President of the United States; If he approve he shall sign it, but if not he shall return it, with his Objections to that House in which it shall have originated, who shall enter the Objections at large on their Journal, and proceed to reconsider it. If after such Reconsideration two thirds of that House shall agree to pass the Bill, it shall be sent, together with the Objections, to the other House, by which it shall likewise be reconsidered, and if approved by two thirds of that House, it shall become a Law. But in all such Cases the Votes of both Houses shall be determined by Yeas and Nays, and the Names of the Persons voting for and against the Bill shall be entered on the Journal of each House respectively. If any Bill shall not be returned by the President within ten Days (Sundays excepted) after it shall have been presented to him, the Same shall be a Law, in like Manner as if he had signed it, unless the Congress by their Adjournment prevent its Return, in which Case it shall not be a Law.

Every Order, Resolution, or Vote to which the Concurrence of the Senate and House of Representatives may be necessary (except on a question of Adjournment) shall be presented to the President of the United States; and before the Same shall take Effect, shall be approved by him, or being disapproved by him, shall be repassed by two thirds of the Senate and House of Representatives, according to the Rules and Limitations prescribed in the Case of a Bill.

*Section 8.* The Congress shall have Power To lay and collect Taxes, Duties, Imposts and Excises, to pay the Debts and provide for the common Defence and general Welfare of the United States; but all Duties, Imposts and Excises shall be uniform throughout the United States;

To borrow Money on the Credit of the United States;

To regulate Commerce with foreign Nations, and among the several States, and with the Indian Tribes;

To establish an uniform Rule of Naturalization, and uniform Laws on the subject of Bankruptcies throughout the United States;

To coin Money, regulate the Value thereof, and of foreign Coin, and fix the Standard of Weights and Measures;

To provide for the Punishment of counterfeiting the securities and current Coin of the United States;

To establish Post Offices and post Roads;

To promote the Progress of Science and useful Arts, by securing for limited Times to Authors and Inventors the exclusive Right to their respective Writings and Discoveries;

To constitute Tribunals inferior to the supreme Court;

To define and punish Piracies and Felonies committed on the high Seas, and Offences against the Law of Nations;

To declare War, grant Letters of Marque and Reprisal, and make Rules concerning Captures on Land and Water;

To raise and support Armies, but no Appropriation of Money to that Use shall be for a longer Term than two Years;

To provide and maintain a Navy;

To make Rules for the Government and Regulation of the land and naval Forces;

To provide for calling forth the Militia to execute the Laws of the Union, suppress Insurrections and repel Invasions;

To provide for organizing, arming, and disciplining, the Militia, and for governing such Part of them as may be employed in the Service of the United States, reserving to the States respectively, the Appointment of the Officers, and the Authority of training the Militia according to the discipline prescribed by Congress;

To exercise exclusive Legislation in all Cases whatsoever, over such District (not exceeding ten Miles square) as may, by Cession of particular States, and the Acceptance of Congress, become the Seat of the Government of the United States, and to exercise like Authority over all Places purchased by the Consent of the Legislature of the State in which the Same shall be for the Erection of Forts, Magazines, Arsenals, dock-Yards, and other needful Buildings;-And

To make all Laws which shall be necessary and proper for carrying into Execution the foregoing Powers, and all other Powers vested by this Constitution in the Government of the United States, or in any Department or Officer thereof.

*Section 9.* The Migration of Importation of such Persons as any of the States now existing shall think proper to admit, shall not be prohibited by the Congress prior to the Year one thousand eight hundred and eight, but a Tax or duty may be imposed on such Importation, not exceeding ten dollars for each Person.

The Privilege of the Writ of Habeas Corpus shall not be suspended, unless when in Cases of Rebellion or Invasion the public Safety may require it.

No Bill of Attainder or ex post facto Law shall be passed.

No Capitation, or other direct, Tax shall be laid, unless in Proportion to the Census or Enumeration herein before directed to be taken.

No Tax or Duty shall be laid on Articles exported from any State.

No preference shall be given by any Regulation of Commerce or Revenue to the Ports of one State over those of another: nor shall Vessels bound to, or from, one State, be obliged to enter, clear, or pay Duties in another.

No money shall be drawn from the Treasury, but in Consequence of Appropriations made by Law; and a regular Statement and Account of the Receipts and Expenditures of all public Money shall be published from time to time.

No Title of Nobility shall be granted by the United States: And no Person holding any Office of Profit or Trust under them, shall, without the Consent of the Congress, accept of any present, Emolument, Office, or Title, of any kind whatever, from any King, Prince, or foreign State.

*Section 10.* No State shall enter into any Treaty, Alliance, or Confederation; grant Letters of Marque and Reprisal; coin Money; emits Bills of Credit; make any Thing but gold and silver Coin a Tender in Payment of Debts; pass any Bill of Attainder, ex post facto Law, or Law impairing the Obligation of Contracts, or grant any Title of Nobility.

No State shall, without the Consent of the Congress, lay any Imposts or Duties on Imports or Exports, except what may be absolutely necessary for executing it's inspection Laws: and the net Produce of all Duties and Imposts, laid by any State on Imports or Exports, shall be for the Use of the Treasury of the United States; and all such Laws shall be subject to the Revision and Control of the Congress.

No State shall, without the Consent of the Congress, lay any Duty of Tonnage, keep Troops, or Ships of War in time of Peace, enter into any Agreement or Compact with another State, or with a foreign Power, or engage in War, unless actually invaded, or in such imminent Danger as will not admit of delay.

**Article II**

*Section 1.* The executive Power shall be vested in a President of the United States of America. He shall hold his Office during the Term of four Years, and, together with the Vice President, chosen for the same term, be elected, as follows

Each State shall appoint, in such Manner as the Legislature thereof may direct, a Number of Electors, equal to the whole Number of Senators and Representatives to which the State may be entitled in the Congress: but no Senator or Representative, or Person holding an Office of Trust or Profit under the United States, shall be appointed an Elector.

The Electors shall meet in their respective States, and vote by Ballot for two Persons, of whom one at least shall not be an Inhabitant of the same State with themselves. And they shall make a List of all the Persons voted for, and of the Number of Votes for each; which List they shall sign and certify, and transmit sealed to the Seat of the Government of the United States, directed to the President of the Senate. The President of the Senate shall, in the Presence of the Senate and House of Representatives, open all the Certificates, and the Votes shall then be counted. The Person having the greatest Number of Votes shall be the President, if such Number be a majority of the whole Number of Electors appointed; and if there be no more than one who have such Majority, and have an equal Number of Votes, then the House of Representatives shall immediately choose by Ballot one of them for President: and if no Person have a Majority, then from the five highest on the List the said House shall in like Manner choose the President. But in choosing the President, the Votes shall be taken by the states, the Representation from each State having one Vote; A quorum for this Purpose shall consist of a Member or Members from two thirds of the States, and a Majority of all the States shall be necessary to a Choice. In every Case, after the Choice of the President, the Person having the greatest Number of Votes of the Electors shall be the Vice President. But if there should remain two or more who have equal Votes, the Senate shall choose from them by Ballot the Vice President.

The Congress may determine the Time of choosing the Electors, and the Day on which they shall give their Votes; which Day shall be the same throughout the United States.

No Person except a natural born Citizen, or a Citizen of the United States, at the time of the Adoption of this Constitution, shall be eligible to the Office of President; neither shall any Person be eligible to that Office who shall not have attained to the Age of thirty five Years, and been fourteen Years a Resident within the United States.

In Case of the Removal of the President from Office, or of his Death, Resignation, or Inability to discharge the Powers and Duties of the said Office, the Same shall devolve on the Vice President, and the Congress may by Law provide for the Case of Removal, Death, Resignation or Inability, both of the President and Vice President, declaring what Officer shall then act as President, and such Officer shall act accordingly, until the Disability be removed, or a President shall be elected.

The President shall, at stated Times, receive for his Services, a Compensation, which shall neither be increased nor diminished during the Period for which he shall have been elected, and he shall not receive within that Period any other Emolument from the United States, or any of them.

Before he enter on the Execution of his Office, he shall take the following Oath or Affirmation:-"I do solemnly swear (or affirm) that I will faithfully execute the Office of President of the United States, and will to the best of my Ability, preserve, protect and defend the Constitution of the United States."

*Section 2.* The President shall be Commander in Chief of the Army and Navy of the United States, and of the Militia of the several States, when called into the actual Service of the United States; he may require the Opinion, in writing, of the principal Officer in each of the executive Departments, upon any Subject relating to the Duties of their respective Offices, and he shall have Power to grant Reprieves and Pardons for Offences against the United States, except in Cases of Impeachment.

He shall have Power, by and with the Advice and Consent of the Senate, to make Treaties, provided two thirds of the Senators present concur; and he shall nominate, and by and with the Advice and Consent of the Senate, shall appoint Ambassadors, other public Ministers and Consuls, Judges of the supreme Court, and all other Officers of the United States, whose Appointments are not herein otherwise provided for, and which shall be established by Law: but the Congress may by Law vest the Appointment of such inferior Officers, as they think proper, in the President alone, in the Courts of Law, or in the Heads of Departments.

The President shall have Power to fill up all Vacancies that may happen during the Recess of the Senate, by granting Commissions which shall expire at the End of their next Session.

*Section 3.* He shall from time to time give to the Congress Information of the State of the Union, and recommend to their Consideration such Measures as he shall judge necessary and expedient; he may, on extraordinary Occasions, convene both Houses, or either of them, and in Case of Disagreement between them, with Respect to the Time of Adjournment, he may adjourn them to such Time as he shall think proper; he shall receive Ambassadors and other public Ministers; he shall take Care that the Laws be faithfully executed, and shall Commission all the Officers of the United States.

*Section 4.* The President, Vice President, and all civil Officers of the United States, shall be removed from Office on Impeachment for, and Conviction of, Treason, Bribery, or other High Crimes and Misdemeanors.

**Article III**
*Section 1.* The judicial Power of the United States, shall be vested in one supreme Court, and in such inferior Courts as the Congress may from time to time ordain and establish. The Judges, both of the supreme and inferior Courts, shall hold their Offices during good Behaviour, and shall, at stated Times, receive for their Services, a Compensation, which shall not be diminished during their Continuance in Office.

*Section 2.* The judicial Power shall extend to all Cases, in Law and Equity, arising under this Constitution, the Laws of the United States, and Treaties made, or which shall be made, under their Authority;-to all Cases affecting Ambassadors, other public Ministers and Consuls;-to all Cases of admiralty and maritime Jurisdiction;-to Controversies to which the United States shall be a Party;-to Controversies between two or more States; between a State and Citizens of another state;-between Citizens of different States;-between Citizens of the same State claiming Lands under Grants of different States, and between a State, or the Citizens thereof, and foreign States, Citizens or Subjects.

In all Cases affecting Ambassadors, other public Ministers and Consuls, and those in which a State shall be Party, the supreme Court shall have original Jurisdiction. In all the other Cases before mentioned, the supreme Court shall have appellate Jurisdiction, both as to Law and Fact, with such Exceptions, and under such Regulations as the Congress shall make.

The Trial of all Crimes, except in Cases of Impeachment, shall be by Jury; and such Trial shall be held in the State where the said Crimes shall have been committed; but when not committed within any State, the Trial shall be at such Place or Places as the Congress may by Law have directed.

*Section 3.* Treason against the United States, shall consist only in levying War against them, or in adhering to their Enemies, giving them Aid and Comfort. No Person shall be convicted of Treason unless on the Testimony of two Witnesses to the same overt Act, or on Confession in open Court.

The Congress shall have Power to declare the Punishment of Treason, but no Attainder of Treason shall work Corruption of Blood, or Forfeiture except during the Life of the Person attainted.

**Article IV**

*Section 1.* Full Faith and Credit shall be given in each State to the public Acts, Records, and judicial Proceedings of every other State. And the Congress may be general Laws prescribe the Manner in which such Acts, Records and Proceedings shall be proved, and the Effect thereof.

*Section 2.* The Citizens of each State shall be entitled to all Privileges and Immunities of Citizens in the several States.

A Person charged in any State with Treason, Felony, or other Crime, who shall flee from Justice, and be found in another State, shall on Demand of the executive Authority of the State from which he fled, be delivered up, to be removed to the State having Jurisdiction of the Crime.

No Person held to Service or Labour in one State, under the Laws thereof, escaping into another, shall, in Consequence of any Law or Regulation therein, be discharged from such Service or Labour, but shall be delivered up on Claim of the Party to whom such Service or Labour may be due.

*Section 3.* New States may be admitted by the Congress into this Union; but no new State shall be formed or erected within the Jurisdiction of any other State; nor any State be formed by the Junction of two or more States, or Parts of States, without the Consent of the Legislatures of the States concerned as well as of the Congress.

The Congress shall have Power to dispose of and make all needful Rules and Regulations respecting the Territory or other Property belonging to the United States; and nothing in this Constitution shall be so construed as to Prejudice any Claims of the United States, or of any particular State.

*Section 4.* The United States shall guarantee to every State in this Union a Republican Form of Government, and shall protect each of them against Invasion; and on Application of the Legislature, or of the Executive (when the Legislature cannot be convened) against domestic Violence.

**Article V**

The Congress, whenever two thirds of both Houses shall deem it necessary, shall propose Amendments to this Constitution, or, on the Application of the Legislatures of two thirds of the several States, shall call a Convention for proposing Amendments, which, in either Case, shall be valid to all Intents and Purposes, as Part of this Constitution, when ratified by the Legislatures of three fourths of the several States, or by Conventions in three fourths thereof, as the one or the other Mode of Ratification may be proposed by the Congress; Provided that no Amendment which may be made prior to the Year One Thousand eight hundred and eight shall in any Manner affect the first and fourth Clauses in the Ninth Section of the first Article; and that no State, without its Consent, shall be deprived of its equal Suffrage in the Senate.

**Article VI**

All Debts contracted and Engagements entered into, before the Adoption of this Constitution, shall be as valid against the United States under this Constitution, as under the Confederation.

This Constitution, and the Laws of the United States which shall be made in Pursuance thereof; and all Treaties made, or which shall be made, under the Authority of the United States, shall be the supreme Law of the Land; and the Judges in every State shall be bound thereby, any Thing in the Constitution or Laws of any State to the Contrary notwithstanding.

The Senators and Representatives before mentioned, and the Members of the several State Legislatures, and all executive and judicial Officers, both of the United States and of the several States, shall be bound by Oath or Affirmation, to support this Constitution; but no religious Test shall ever be required as a Qualification to any Office or public Trust under the United States.

## Article VII

The Ratification of the Conventions of nine States, shall be sufficient for the Establishment of this Constitution between the States so ratifying the Same.

## AMENDMENTS TO THE CONSTITUTION

*(The first ten Amendments were ratified Dec. 15, 1791, and form what is known as the Bill of Rights.)*

## Amendment 1

Congress shall make no law respecting an establishment of religion, or prohibiting the free exercise thereof; or abridging the freedom of speech, or of the press, or the right of the people peaceably to assemble, and to petition the Government for a redress of grievances.

## Amendment 2

A well regulated Militia, being necessary to the security of a free State, the right of the people to keep and bear Arms, shall not be infringed.

## Amendment 3

No Soldier shall, in time of peace be quartered in any house, without the consent of the Owner, nor in time of war, but in a manner to be prescribed by law.

## Amendment 4

The right of the people to be secure in their persons, houses, papers, and effects, against unreasonable searches and seizures, shall not be violated, and no Warrants shall issue, but upon probable cause, supported by Oath or affirmation, and particularly describing the place to be searched, and the persons or things to be seized.

## Amendment 5

No person shall be held to answer for a capital, or otherwise infamous crime, unless on a presentment or indictment of a Grand Jury, except in cases arising in the land or naval forces, or in the Militia, when in actual service in time of War or public danger; nor shall any person be subject for the same offence to be twice put in jeopardy of life or limb; nor shall be compelled in any criminal case to be a witness against himself, nor be deprived of life, liberty, or property, without due process of law; nor shall private property be taken for public use, without just compensation.

## Amendment 6

In all criminal prosecutions, the accused shall enjoy the right to a speedy and public trial, by an impartial jury of the State and district wherein the crime shall have been committed, which district shall have been previously ascertained by law, and to be informed of the nature and cause of the accusation; to be confronted with the witnesses against him; to have compulsory process for obtaining witnesses in his favor, and to have the Assistance of Counsel for his defence.

## Amendment 7

In Suits at common law, where the value in controversy shall exceed twenty dollars, the right of trial by jury shall be preserved, and no fact tried by a jury, shall be otherwise re-examined in any Court of the United States, than according to the rules of the common law.

## Amendment 8

Excessive bail shall not be required, nor excessive fines imposed, nor cruel and unusual punishments inflicted.

## Amendment 9

The enumeration in the Constitution, of certain rights, shall not be construed to deny or disparage others retained by the people.

## Amendment 10

The powers not delegated to the United States by the Constitution, nor prohibited by it to the States, are reserved to the States respectively, or to the people.

## Amendment 11

*(Ratified Feb. 7, 1795)*

The Judicial power of the United States shall not be construed to extend to any suit in law or equity, commenced or prosecuted against one of the United States by Citizens of another State, or by Citizens or Subjects of any Foreign State.

## Amendment 12

*(Ratified July 27, 1804)*

The Electors shall meet in their respective States and vote by ballot for President and Vice President, one of whom, at least, shall not be an inhabitant of the same State with themselves; they shall name in their ballots the person voted for as President, and in distinct ballots the person voted for as Vice President, and they shall make distinct lists of all persons voted for as President, and of all persons voted for as Vice President, and of the number of votes for each, which lists they shall sign and certify, and transmit sealed to the seat of the government of the United States, directed to the President of the Senate;-The President of the Senate shall, in the presence of the Senate and House of Representatives, open all the certificates and the votes shall then be counted;-The person having the greatest number of votes for President, shall be the President, if such number be a majority of the whole number of Electors appointed; and if no person have such majority, then from the persons having the highest numbers not exceeding three on the list of those voted for as President, the House of Representatives shall choose immediately, by ballot, the President. But in choosing the President, the votes shall be taken by states, the representation from each state having one vote; a quorum for this purpose shall consist of a member or members from two-thirds of the states, and a majority of all the states shall be necessary to a choice. And if the House of Representatives shall not choose a President whenever the right of choice shall devolve upon them, before the fourth day of March next following, then the Vice

President shall act as President, as in the case of the death or other constitutional disability of the President.-The person having the greatest number of votes as Vice President, shall be the Vice President, if such number be a majority of the whole number of Electors appointed, and if no person have a majority, then from the two highest numbers on the list, the Senate shall choose the Vice President; a quorum for the purpose shall consist of two-thirds of the whole number of Senators, and a majority of the whole number shall be necessary to a choice. But no person constitutionally ineligible to the office of President shall be eligible to that of Vice President of the United States.

## Amendment 13

*(Ratified Dec. 6, 1865)*

*Section 1.* Neither Slavery, nor involuntary servitude, except as a punishment for crime whereof the party shall have been duly convicted, shall exist within the United States, or any place subject to their jurisdiction.

*Section 2.* Congress shall have power to enforce this article by appropriate legislation.

## Amendment 14

*(Ratified July 9, 1868)*

*Section 1.* All persons born or naturalized in the United States, and subject to the jurisdiction thereof, are citizens of the United States and of the State wherein they reside. No State shall make or enforce any law which shall abridge the privileges or immunities of citizens of the United States; nor shall any State deprive any person of life, liberty, or property, without due process of law; nor deny to any person within its jurisdiction the equal protection of the laws.

*Section 2.* Representatives shall be apportioned among the several States according to their respective numbers, counting the whole number of persons in each State, excluding Indians not taxed. But when the right to vote at any election for the choice of electors for President and Vice President of the United States, Representatives in Congress, the Executive and Judicial officers of a State, or the members of the Legislature thereof, is denied to any of the male inhabitants of such State, being twenty-one years of age, and citizens of the United States, or in any way abridged, except for participation in rebellion, or other crime, the basis of representation therein shall be reduced in the proportion which the number of such male citizens shall bear to the whole number of male citizens twenty-one years of age in such State.

*Section 3.* No person shall be a Senator or Representative in Congress, or elector of President and Vice President, or hold any office, civil or military, under the United States, or under any State, who, having previously taken an oath, as a member of Congress, or as an officer of the United States, or as a member of any State legislature, or as an executive or judicial officer of any State, to support the Constitution of the United States, shall have engaged in insurrection or rebellion against the same, or given aid or comfort to the enemies thereof. But Congress may by a vote of two-thirds of each House, remove such disability.

*Section 4.* The validity of the public debt of the United States, authorized by law, including debts incurred for payment of pensions and bounties for services in suppressing insurrection or rebellion, shall not be questioned. But neither the United States nor any State shall assume or pay any debt or obligation incurred in aid of insurrection or rebellion against the United States, or any claim for the loss or emancipation of any slave; but all such debts, obligations and claims shall be held illegal and void.

*Section 5.* The Congress shall have power to enforce, by appropriate legislation, the provision of this article.

## Amendment 15
*(Ratified Feb. 3, 1870)*
*Section 1.* The right of citizens of the United States to vote shall not be denied or abridged by the United States or by any State on account of race, color or previous condition of servitude.

*Section 2.* The Congress shall have power to enforce this article by appropriate legislation.

## Amendment 16
*(Ratified Feb. 3, 1913)*
The Congress shall have power to lay and collect taxes on incomes, from whatever source derived, without apportionment among the several States, and without regard to any census or enumeration.

## Amendment 17

*(Ratified April 8, 1913)*

The Senate of the United States shall be composed of two Senators from each State, elected by the people thereof for six years; and each Senator shall have one vote. The electors in each State shall have the qualifications requisite for electors of the most numerous branch of the State legislatures.

When vacancies happen in the representation of any State in the Senate, the executive authority of such State shall issue writs of election to fill such vacancies: Provided, That the legislature of any State may empower the executive thereof to make temporary appointments until the people fill the vacancies by election as the legislature may direct.

This amendment shall not be so construed as to affect the election or term of any Senator chosen before it becomes valid as part of the Constitution.

## Amendment 18

*(Ratified Jan. 16, 1919)*

*Section 1.* After one year from the ratification of this article the manufacture, sale, or transportation of intoxicating liquors within, the importation thereof into, or the exportation thereof from the United States and all territory subject to the jurisdiction thereof for beverage purposes is hereby prohibited.

*Section 2.* The Congress and the several States shall have concurrent power to enforce this article by appropriate legislation.

*Section 3.* This article shall be inoperative unless it shall have been ratified as an amendment to the Constitution by the legislatures of the several States, as provided in the Constitution, within seven years from the date of the submission hereof to the States by the Congress.

## Amendment 19

*(Ratified Aug. 18, 1920)*

The right of citizens of the United States to vote shall not be denied or abridged by the United States or by any State on account of sex.

Congress shall have power to enforce this article by appropriate legislation.

## Amendment 20

*(Ratified Jan. 23, 1933)*

*Section 1.* The terms of the President and Vice President shall end at noon on the 20th day of January, and the terms of Senators and Representatives at noon on the third day of January, of the years in which such terms would have ended if this article had not been ratified; and the terms of their successors shall then begin.

*Section 2.* The Congress shall assemble at least once in every year, and such meeting shall begin at noon on the third day of January, unless they shall by law appoint a different day.

*Section 3.* If, at the time fixed for the beginning of the term of the President, the President elect shall have died, the Vice President elect shall become President. If a President shall not have been chosen before the time fixed for the beginning of his term, or if the President elect shall have failed to qualify, then the Vice President elect shall act as President until a President shall have qualified; and the Congress may by law provide for the case wherein neither a President elect nor a Vice President elect shall have qualified, declaring who shall then act as President, or the manner in which one who is to act shall be selected, and such person shall act accordingly until a President or Vice President shall have qualified.

*Section 4.* The Congress may by law provide for the case of the death of any of the persons from whom the House of Representatives may choose a President whenever the right of choice shall have devolved upon them, and for the case of the death of any of the persons from whom the Senate may choose a Vice President whenever the right of choice shall have devolved upon them.

*Section 5.* Sections 1 and 2 shall take effect on the 15th day of October following the ratification of this article.

*Section 6.* This article shall be inoperative unless it shall have been ratified as an amendment to the Constitution by the legislatures of three-fourths of the several States within seven years from the date of its submission.

## Amendment 21

*(Ratified Dec. 5, 1933)*

*Section 1.* The eighteenth article of amendment to the Constitution of the United States is hereby repealed.

*Section 2.* The transportation or importation into any State, Territory, or possession of the United States for delivery or use therein of intoxicating liquors, in violation of the laws thereof, is hereby prohibited.

*Section 3.* This article shall be inoperative unless it shall have been ratified as an amendment to the Constitution by conventions in the several States, as provided in the Constitution, within seven years from the date of the submission hereof to the States by the Congress.

## Amendment 22
*(Ratified Feb. 27, 1951)*
*Section 1.* No person shall be elected to the office of the President more than twice, and no person who has held the office of President, or acted as President, for more than two years of a term to which some other person was elected President shall be elected to the office of the President more than once. But this Article shall not apply to any person holding the office of President when this Article was proposed by the Congress, and shall not prevent any person who may be holding the office of President, or acting as President, during the term within which this Article becomes operative from holding the office of President or acting as President during the remainder of such term.

*Section 2.* This article shall be inoperative unless it shall have been ratified as an amendment to the Constitution by the legislatures of three-fourths of the several States within seven years from the date of its submission to the States by the Congress.

## Amendment 23
*(Ratified March 29, 1961)*
*Section 1.* The District constituting the seat of Government of the United States shall appoint in such manner as the Congress may direct:

A number of electors of President and Vice President equal to the whole number of Senators and Representatives in Congress to which the District would be entitled if it were a State, but in no event more than the least populous State; they shall be in addition to those appointed by the States, but they shall be considered, for the purposes of the election of President and Vice President, to be electors appointed by a State; and they shall meet in the District and perform such duties as provided by the twelfth article of amendment.

*Section 2.* The Congress shall have power to enforce this article by appropriate legislation.

## Amendment 24
*(Ratified Jan. 23, 1964)*

*Section 1.* The right of citizens of the United States to vote in any primary or other election for President or Vice President, for electors for President or Vice President, or for Senator or Representative in Congress, shall not be denied or abridged by the United States or any State by reason of failure to pay any poll tax or other tax.

*Section 2.* The Congress shall have power to enforce this article by appropriate legislation.

## Amendment 25
*(Ratified Feb. 10, 1967)*

*Section 1.* In case of the removal of the President from office or of his death or resignation, the Vice President shall become President.

*Section 2.* Whenever there is a vacancy in the office of the Vice President, the President shall nominate a Vice President who shall take office upon confirmation by a majority vote of both Houses of Congress.

*Section 3.* Whenever the President transmits to the President pro tempore of the Senate and the Speaker of the House of Representatives his written declaration that he is unable to discharge the powers and duties of his office, and until he transmits to them a written declaration to the contrary, such powers and duties shall be discharged by the Vice President as Acting President.

*Section 4.* Whenever the Vice President and a majority of either the principal officers of the executive departments or of such other body as Congress may by law provide, transmit to the President pro tempore of the Senate and the Speaker of the House of Representatives their written declaration that the President is unable to discharge the powers and duties of his office, the Vice President shall immediately assume the powers and duties of the office as Acting President.

Thereafter, when the President transmits to the President pro tempore of the Senate and the Speaker of the House of Representatives his written declaration that no inability exists, he shall resume the powers and duties of his office unless the Vice President and a majority of either the principal officers of the executive department or of such other body as Congress may by law provide, transmit within four days to the President pro tempore of the Senate and the Speaker of the House of Representatives their written declaration that the President is unable to discharge the powers and duties of his office. Thereupon Congress shall decide the issue, assembling within forty-eight hours for that purpose if not in session. If the Congress, within twenty-one days after receipt of the latter written declaration, or, if Congress is not in session, within twenty-one days after Congress is required to assemble, determines by two-thirds vote of both Houses that the President is unable to discharge the powers and duties of his office, the Vice President shall continue to discharge the same as Acting President; otherwise, the President shall resume the powers and duties of his office.

## Amendment 26
*(Ratified July 1, 1971)*
*Section 1.* The right of citizens of the United States, who are 18 years of age or older, to vote shall not be denied or abridged by the United States or by any State on account of age.

*Section 2.* The Congress shall have power to enforce this article by appropriate legislation.

## Amendment 27
*(Ratified May 7, 1992)*
No law, varying the compensation for the services of the Senators and Representatives, shall take effect until an election of Representatives shall have intervened.

# 13 An Overview of Our System of Government

The United States is a republic. A republic is a government run by the people through their representatives. These representatives are elected to office by United States citizens, who are allowed to vote for their choice of representatives. Some people call this the "democratic process". President Abraham Lincoln termed this a government "of the people, by the people and for the people". There are two major political parties in the United States, the Republicans and the Democrats. The minimum voting age in the United States is eighteen.

**There are four levels of government in the United States.**

1. **Federal Government**
   Headquarters are in our country's capital, Washington, DC.
   The Chief Executive of the Federal Government is the President.

2. **State Government**
   Headquarters are in the capital of each of the fifty states.
   The Chief Executive of the State is called the Governor.

3. **County Government**
   Headquarters are in the county seat in each county within the State.

4. **Local Government**
   Headquarters are in each township, city and municipality in the United States. The Chief Executive of each city or town is usually called the Mayor.

This book will address the structure of the Federal Government. You should have some basic knowledge of your State, County and municipal or local government, as well.

**The three branches of the Federal Government are:**

- Legislative
- Executive
- Judicial

The **Legislative branch** makes the laws. It is called the Congress and consists of the Senate and the House of Representatives. The Senate has one hundred senators, two from each State. Senators are elected by the people of their State to serve for a six-year term. There is no limit on the amount of years they can be re-elected to serve. Senators must be at least thirty years old, and must be citizens of the United States. If a Senator was not born in the U.S., he or she must have resided in the United States for nine years as a U.S. citizen before his or her election. Presiding over the Senate is the Vice President of the United States.

The House of Representatives is the other half of the Legislative branch of government. It is made up of four hundred thirty five representatives, also known as Congressmen, elected by the people of their State. The State's population determines the number of representatives from each State. The population is counted every ten years in an official census. A representative serves for a term of two years. There is no limit on the number of years they can be re-elected or serve. Representatives must be at least twenty-five years of age and must be citizens of the United States. If a Representative was not born in the U.S., he or she must have resided in the United States for seven years as a U.S. citizen before his or her election. Presiding over the House of Representatives is the Speaker of the House.

The Congress (Legislative Branch) makes the laws. It meets in our Capitol in Washington, DC. Laws start out as bills that are proposed by either the Senate or the House of Representatives. The bill is usually studied and debated by various committees of the Legislature. A law must pass by a majority vote in both the Senate and House of Representatives. It then goes to the President of the United States for signature. It only becomes a law if the President signs. If he refuses to sign, or vetoes the bill, it can still become a law by a two third's majority vote in both the Senate and House of Representatives.

The **Executive Branch** enforces the laws and is made up of the President, the Vice President, fourteen cabinet members (and departments), selected by the President to help him. The President is elected by a group of electors called the Electoral College. As President, he or she also serves as Commander in Chief of the U.S. Military. The President must be at least thirty-five years old and must have been born in the United States. He must have resided in the United States for at least fourteen years prior to his election. The President serves for a term of four years and cannot be elected for more than two consecutive terms. Elections are held in November, and the Presidential Inauguration is held the following January. Our first President, "the Father of Our Country", was George Washing-ton. He was also the first Commander in Chief of the U.S. Military. Our current President is William (Bill) Clinton. The President of the United States' official home is the White House in Washington, DC.

The Vice President needs to have the same qualifications as the President since he or she takes over the duties of the President if the President dies, resigns, or is unable to carry out his or her duties. Our current Vice President is Albert Gore.

The Cabinet members are the President's assistants and advisers, and are chosen directly by the President. The Senate, however, must approve their appointment. The Cabinet members hold office until they resign, or until a new President is elected.

The order of presidential succession is as follows:

1.  The Vice President
2.  Speaker of the House
3.  President pro tempore of the Senate
4.  Secretary of State
5.  Secretary of the Treasury
6.  Continues to 16th—the Secretary of Education.

The **Judicial Branch** interprets the law. At the head of the Judicial Branch is the Supreme Court, the highest court in the United States. The Supreme Court is made up of nine justices or judges. One of them is appointed Chief Justice. Our current Chief Justice is William Rehnquist. They are all appointed by the President and serve for life, or good behavior. The other Federal Courts fall under the jurisdiction of the Supreme Court.

The three branches of government were created and designed to protect our freedom in a system called "checks and balances". This way, the powers of the Federal government are divided and balanced so that no one branch can control the people or the other branches. This system is the called the "separation of powers". Our Founding Fathers had experienced the abuses of authority that the English government had inflicted on the colonies, and wanted to prevent the same abuses from occurring in America.

# 14 American Holidays and Symbols

**Some of the more important dates celebrated by Americans are:**

| | |
|---|---|
| January 1 | New Year's Day |
| Third Monday in January | Martin Luther King, Jr. Day |
| February 12 | Lincoln's Birthday |
| February 14 | St. Valentine's Day |
| February 22 | Washington's Birthday |
| Third Monday in February | Presidents' Day |
| Second Sunday in May | Mother's Day |
| Fourth Monday in May | Memorial Day |
| June 14 | Flag Day |
| Third Sunday in June | Father's Day |
| July 4 | Independence Day |
| First Monday in September | Labor Day |
| October 12 | Columbus Day |
| October 31 | Halloween |
| The first Tuesday after the first Monday in November | Election Day |
| November 11 | Veterans Day |
| Fourth Thursday in November | Thanksgiving |

**New Years Day**—A legal holiday in all states. It originated in Roman times, when Janus, a Roman deity with two faces, reflected on the past and looked forward to the future.

**Martin Luther King Jr.'s Birthday**—Became a legal public holiday in 1986. Honors our late civil rights leader, Martin Luther King.

**Lincoln's Birthday**—First observed in 1866 when both Houses of Congress gathered to memorialize the assassinated President, Abraham Lincoln. It is a legal holiday in many states.

**St. Valentine's Day**—A celebration of two martyrs from the third century, who were both named St. Valentine. There are many opinions as to why this day is associated with lovers, but no certain answers.

**Washington's Birthday**—Began in 1796 to celebrate the birthday of our first President, George Washington. It is a legal holiday throughout the U.S.

**Presidents' Day**—Recently, we have begun to jointly acknowledge Presidents of the United States on this day.

**Mother's Day**—A day to honor all mothers. Originally proposed by Anna Jarvis of Philadelphia in 1907.

**Memorial Day**—Also known as Decoration Day. A day dedicated to the memory of all those who died in war. Ordered by General John A. Logan, Commander in Chief of the Grand Army of the Republic in 1868. It is a legal holiday in most states.

**Flag Day**—Commemorates the day the Continental Congress adopted the Stars and Stripes as the U.S. flag on June 14, 1777. It is only a legal holiday in Pennsylvania, but is observed throughout the United States.

**Father's Day**—A day to honor all fathers. First observed on June 19, 1910.

**Independence Day**—The day the U.S. adopted the Declaration of Independence (from England) in 1776. It is a legal holiday in all states.

**Labor Day**—A day set aside to honor all American workers. It was first celebrated in New York in 1882, under the sponsorship of the Central Labor Union. It is a legal holiday in all states.

**Columbus Day**—Commemorates the discovery of America by Christopher Columbus in 1492. It is a legal holiday in many states.

**Halloween**—On the Eve of All Saints Day. A day for children in the U.S. to dress up in costumes for masquerades.

**Election Day**—The date chosen by Act of Congress in 1845 to elect the President of the United States. State elections are usually held on this day, as well. This is a legal holiday in some states.

**Veteran's Day**—Also called Armistice Day until 1954. It commemorates the 1918 signing of the Armistice, ending World War I. It honors all men and women who have served in America's armed forces.

**Thanksgiving**—Observed nationally since 1941 by Act of Congress, as a day of giving thanks. In America it is believed that the American Colonists first celebrated Thanksgiving in 1621, when ordered by Governor Bradford of Plymouth Colony in New England.


## THE AMERICAN FLAG

The first American flag was reportedly designed and sewn by Betsy Ross in 1776. Our Flag is red, white and blue, for courage, truth and justice, respectively. Each of the thirteen red and white stripes represents one colony. Each white star represents one of the fifty states in the Union. Hawaii and Alaska are the forty-ninth and fiftieth states. We show our loyalty to the flag with the following "Pledge of Allegiance", authored by Francis Bellamy in 1892. The phrase "under God" was not added until 1954.

> *I pledge allegiance to the flag*
> *of the United States of America*
> *And to the Republic for which it stands*
> *One nation under God, indivisible*
> *With liberty and justice for all*


## THE STATUE OF LIBERTY

The Statute was given to the United States by France to commemorate the alliance of the two countries in the American Revolution. President Grover Cleveland accepted the statue on October 28, 1886. The Statue of Liberty sits on Liberty Island in New York Harbor. It is a 152-foot high female figure made of steel reinforced copper. The right hand holds a torch while the left carries a table with the inscription: "July IV MDCCLXXVI".

In 1972 President Nixon dedicated the American Museum of Immigration, located at the base of the Statue.

## OUR NATIONAL ANTHEM

The *"Star-Spangled Banner"* is our national anthem. It was written by Francis Scott Key in 1814, and is sung to the tune *"To Anacreon in Heaven"*. Congress officially made it the National Anthem in 1931. The most popular section of the National Anthem is as follows:

*O say, can you see, by the dawn's early light,*
*What so proudly we hail'd at the twilight's last gleaming?*
*Whose broad stripes and bright stars, thro' the perilous fight,*
*O'er the ramparts we watch'd, were so gallantly streaming?*
*And the rockets' red glare, the bombs bursting in air,*
*Gave proof thro' the night that our flag was still there.*
*O say, does that star-spangled banner yet wave*
*O'er the land of the free and the home of the brave?*

## OUR NATIONAL MOTTO
In God We Trust

## OUR SYMBOL
The Bald Eagle

## OUR CURRENCY
The U.S. Dollar

100 Pennies = $1.00
20 Nickels = $1.00
10 Dimes = $1.00
4 Quarters = $1.00

Our national motto "In God We Trust" first appeared on our coins in 1864.

## THE UNITED NATIONS

The United Nations came into existence in 1945, and in the spring of 1951 it established a permanent home in New York City. The organization is comprised of representatives from most countries around the world. The purpose of the United Nations is to promote peace, security and economic development.

# 15 Presidents of the United States

**George W. Bush is our forty-third President.**

**Our Presidents held office in the following order:**

1. George Washington
2. John Adams
3. Thomas Jefferson
4. James Madison
5. James Monroe
6. John Quincy Adams
7. Andrew Jackson
8. Martin Van Buren
9. William Harrison
10. John Tyler
11. James K. Polk
12. Zachary Taylor
13. Millard Fillmore
14. Franklin Pierce
15. James Buchanan
16. Abraham Lincoln
17. Andrew Johnson
18. Ulysses S. Grant
19. Rutherford B. Hayes
20. James A. Garfield
21. Chester A. Arthur
22. Grover Cleveland
23. Benjamin Harrison
24. Grover Cleveland
25. William McKinley
26. Theodore Roosevelt
27. William H. Taft
28. Woodrow Wilson
29. Warren G. Harding
30. Calvin Coolidge
31. Herbert Hoover
32. Franklin D. Roosevelt
33. Harry S. Truman
34. Dwight D. Eisenhower

35. John F. Kennedy
36. Lyndon B. Johnson
37. Richard M. Nixon
38. Gerald R. Ford
39. James Earl Carter

40. Ronald Reagan
41. George Bush
42. William (Bill) Clinton
43. George W. Bush

# 16 Sample Test Questions and Answers

## QUESTIONS

1.  What are the colors of our flag?_____

2.  How many stars are in our flag? _____

3.  What color are the stars on our flag? _____

4.  What do the stars on the flag mean?_____

5.  How many stripes are on the flag? _____

6.  What color are the stripes? _____

7.  What do the stripes on the flag mean? _____

8.  How many states are there in the Union? _____

9.  What is the 4th of July? _____

10. What is the date of Independence Day?_____

11. From what country did the colonies declare Independence? _____

12. What country did we fight during the Revolutionary War? _____

13. Who was the first President of the United States? _____

14. Who is the President of the United States today?_____

15. Who is the Vice President of the United States?_____

16. Who elects the President of the United States? _____

17. Who becomes President of the United States if the
President should die? _____

18. For how long do we elect the President? _____

19. What is the Constitution? _____

20. Can the Constitution be changed? _____

21. What do we call a change to the Constitution? _____

22. How many changes or amendments
are there to the Constitution? _____

23. How many branches are there in our government? _____

24. What are the three branches of our government? _____

25. What is the legislative branch of our government? _____

26. Who makes the laws in the United States? _____

27. What is Congress? _____

28. What are the duties of Congress? _____

29. Who elects Congress? _____

30. How many senators are there in Congress? _____

31. Can you name the two senators
from your state? _____

32. For how long do we elect each senator? _____

33. How many representatives are there in Congress? _____

34. For how long do we elect the representatives? _____

35. What is the executive branch of our government? _____

36. What is the judicial branch of our government? _____

37. What are the duties of the Supreme Court? _____

38. What is the "Supreme Law of the United States"? _____

39. What is the Bill of Rights? _____

40. What is the capital of your state? _____

41. Who is the current Governor of your state? _____

42. Who becomes President of the United States
    if the President and the Vice President should die? _____

43. Who is the Chief Justice of the Supreme Court? _____

44. Can you name the thirteen original states? _____

45. Who said, "Give me liberty or give me death"? _____

46. Which major countries were our enemies
    during World War II? _____

47. What are the 49th and 50th states of the Union? _____

48. How many terms can a President serve? _____

49. Who was Martin Luther King, Jr.? _____

50. Who is the head of your local government? _____

51. According to the Constitution, a person must meet
    certain requirements  in order to be eligible to become
    President. Name one of these requirements? _____

52. Why are there one hundred Senators in the Senate? _____

53. Who selects the Supreme Court Justice? _____

54. How many Supreme Court Justices are there? _____

55. Why did the Pilgrims come to America? _____

56. What is the head executive of a state government called? _____

57. What is the head executive of a city government called? _____

58. What holiday was celebrated for the first time
    by the American Colonists? _____

59. Who was the main writer of the
    Declaration of Independence? _____

60. When was the Declaration of Independence adopted?_____

61. What is the basic belief of the Declaration
    of Independence? _____

62. What is the national anthem of the United States?_____

63. Who wrote the Star Spangled Banner?_____

64. Where does freedom of speech come from? _____

65. What is the minimum voting age in the United States? _____

66. Who signs bills into law?_____

67. What is the highest court in the United States? _____

68. Who was President during the Civil War? _____

69. What did the Emancipation Proclamation do? _____

70. What special group advises the President? _____

71. Which President is called the "Father of our Country" ? _____

72. What Immigration and Naturalization Service form
    is used to apply to become a naturalized citizen?_____

73. Who helped the pilgrims in America? _____

74. What is the name of the ship that brought
    the Pilgrims to America? _____

75. What were the thirteen original states of the U.S. called? _____

76. Name three rights or freedoms guaranteed
by the Bill or Rights? _____

77. Who has the power to declare war? _____

78. What kind of government does the United States have? _____

79. Which President freed the slaves? _____

80. In what year was the Constitution written? _____

81. What are the first 10 amendments to
the Constitution called? _____

82. What is one main purpose of the United Nations? _____

83. Where does Congress meet? _____

84. Whose rights are guaranteed by the Constitution
and the Bill of Rights? _____

85. What is the introduction to the Constitution called? _____

86. Name one benefit of being a citizen of the United States? _____

87. What is the most important right granted to U.S. Citizens? _____

88. What is the United States Capitol? _____

89. What is the White House? _____

90. Where is the White House located? _____

91. What is the name of the President's official home? _____

92. Name one right guaranteed by the first amendment? _____

93. Who is the Commander in Chief of the U.S. Military? _____

94. Which president was the first
    Commander in Chief of the U.S. Military? _____

95. In what month do we vote for the President? _____

96. In what month is the new President inaugurated? _____

97. How many times may a Congressman be re-elected?_____

98. How many times may a Senator be re-elected?_____

99. What are the two major political parties
    in the U.S. today? _____

100. How many states are there in the United States?_____

**ANSWERS**

1. Red, White and Blue

2. Fifty (50)

3. White

4. One for each state in the union

5. Thirteen (13)

6. Red and White

7. They represent the original thirteen states

8. Fifty (50)

9. Independence Day

10. July 4th

11. England

12. England

13. George Washington

14. George W. Bush

15. Richard B. Cheney

16. The Electoral College

17. Vice President

18. Four years

19. The Supreme law of the land

20. Yes

21. Amendments

22. Twenty seven (27)

23. Three (3)

24. Legislative, Executive and Judicial

25. Congress

26. Congress

27. The Senate and the House of Representatives

28. To make laws

29. The people

30. One hundred (100)

31. Example: Frank Lautenberg, Jon S. Corzine (New Jersey only)

32. Six years

33. Four hundred thirty five (435)

34. Two years

35. The President, Cabinet, and departments under the cabinet members

36. The Supreme Court

37. To interpret laws

38. The Constitution

39. The first ten amendments of the Constitution

40. Example: Trenton (New Jersey only)

41. Example: Richard J. Codey, Acting Governor (New Jersey only)

42. Speaker of the House of Representatives

43. John Roberts

44. Connecticut, New Hampshire, New York, New Jersey, Massachusetts, Pennsylvania, Delaware, Virginia, North Carolina, South Carolina, Georgia, Rhode Island, and Maryland

45. Patrick Henry

46. Germany, Italy, and Japan

47. Alaska and Hawaii

48. Two

49. A civil rights leader

50. (insert local information)

51. Must be a natural born citizen of the U.S.; be at least 35 years old by the time he/she will serve; must have lived in the U.S. for at least fourteen years.

52. Two from each state

53. The President

54. Nine (9)

55. For religious freedom

56. Governor

57. Mayor

58. Thanksgiving

59. Thomas Jefferson

60. July 4, 1776

61. That all men are created equal

62. The Star Spangled Banner

63. Francis Scott Key

64. The Bill of Rights

65. Eighteen (18)

66. The President

67. The Supreme Court

68. Abraham Lincoln

69. Freed many slaves

70. The Cabinet

71. George Washington

72. Form N-400, "Application for Naturalization"

73. The American Indians (Native Americans)

74. The Mayflower

75. The Colonies

76.
   - The right of freedom of speech, press, religion, peaceable assembly and requesting change of government.
   - The right to bear arms (the right to have weapons or own a gun, though subject to certain regulations).
   - The government may not quarter, or house, soldiers in the people's homes during peacetime without the people's consent.
   - The government may not search or take a person's property without a warrant.
   - A person may not be tried twice for the same crime and does not have to testify against him/herself.
   - A person charged with a crime still has some rights, such as the right to a trial and to have a lawyer.
   - The right to trial by jury in most cases.
   - Protects people against excessive or unreasonable fines or cruel and unusual punishment.
   - The people have rights other than those mentioned in the Constitution.
   - Any power not given to the Federal Government by the Constitution is a power of either the State or the people.

77. The Congress

78. Republic

79. Abraham Lincoln

80. 1787

81. The Bill of Rights

82. For countries to discuss and resolve world conflicts

83. In the Capitol in Washington, DC

84. Everyone (citizens and non-citizens living in the U.S.)

85. The Preamble to the Constitution

86. Obtain Federal Government jobs; travel with a U.S. passport; petition for close relatives to come to the U.S. to live.

87. The right to vote

88. The place where Congress meets

89. The President's official home

90. Washington, DC (1600 Pennsylvania Avenue, NW)

91. The White House

92. Freedom of: speech, press, religion, right of petition

93. The President

94. George Washington

95. November

96. January

97. There is no limit

98. There is no limit

99. Democratic and Republican

100. Fifty (50)

# 17 Forms

The following pages contain samples of the documents you will need to file your Application for Naturalization including a cover letter, Form N-400 with instructions and photograph specifications:

*Here is a sample cover letter:*

USCIS
Vermont Service Center
75 Lower Welden Street
St. Albans, Vermont 05479-0001

Re: N-400 Application for Naturalization
My Name: John Jones
My Alien Registration Number: A12 345 678

Dear Immigration Officer:

I am enclosing the following documents to support my Application for Naturalization:

1. Form N-400
2. Copy of my alien registration card (both sides)
3. Biometrics fee of $70.00
4. Photographs
5. Filing fee of $330.00-check #123456

Sincerely,

Your Signature

# Instructions

## What Is the Purpose of This Form?

Form N-400 is an application for U.S. citizenship (naturalization). For more information about the naturalization process and eligibility requirements, please read *A Guide to Naturalization* (M-476). If you do not already have a copy of the *Guide*, you can get a copy from:

- The USCIS website (**www.uscis.gov**);

- The USCIS toll-free forms line at **I-800-870-3676** or

- The USCIS National Customer Service Center (NCSC) at **1-800-375-5283 (TTY: 1-800-767-1833)**.

## Who Should Use This Form?

To use this form you must be at least 18 years old. You must also be **ONE** of the following:

**(1)** A Lawful Permanent Resident for at least five years;

**(2)** A Lawful Permanent Resident for at least three years

### AND

- You have been married to and living with the same U.S. citizen for the last three years,

### AND

- Your spouse has been a U.S. citizen for the last three years;

**(3)** A person who has served in the U.S. Armed Forces,

### AND

- You are a Lawful Permanent Resident with at least three years of U.S. Armed Forces service **and** you are either on active duty or filing within six months of honorable discharge

### OR

- You served during a period of recognized hostilities and enlisted or re-enlisted in the United States (you do not need to be a Lawful Permanent Resident);

**(4)** A member of one of several other groups eligible to apply for naturalization (for example, persons who are nationals but not citizens of the United States). For more information about these groups, please see the *Guide*.

## Who Should Not Use This Form?

In certain cases, a person who was born outside of the United States to U.S. citizen parents is already a citizen and does not need to apply for naturalization. To find out more information about this type of citizenship and whether you should file a Form N-600, "Application for Certificate of Citizenship," read the *Guide*.

Other permanent residents under 18 years of age may be eligible for U.S. citizenship if their U.S. citizen parent or parents file a Form N-600 application in their behalf. For more information, see "Frequently Asked Questions" in the *Guide*.

## When Am I Eligible to Apply?

You may apply for naturalization when you meet **all** the requirements to become a U.S. citizen. The section of the *Guide* called "Who is Eligible for Naturalization" and the Eligibility Worksheet found in the back of the *Guide* are tools to help you determine whether you are eligible to apply for naturalization. You should complete the Worksheet before filling out this Form N-400 application.

If you are applying based on five years as a Lawful Permanent Resident or based on three years as a Lawful Permanent Resident married to a U.S. citizen, you may apply for naturalization up to 90 days before you meet the "continuous residence" requirement. You must meet all other requirements at the time that you file your application with us.

Certain applicants have different English and civics testing requirements based on their age and length of lawful permanent residence **at the time of filing**. If you are over 50 years of age and have lived in the United States as a lawful permanent resident for periods totaling at least 20 years, or if you are over 55 years of age and have lived in the United States as a lawful permanent resident for periods totaling at least 15 years, you do not have to take the English test but you have to take the civics test in the language of your choice.

If you are over 65 years of age and have lived in the United States as a lawful permanent resident for periods totaling at least 20 years, you do not have to take the English test but you have to take a simpler version of the civics test in the language of your choice.

## What Does It Cost to Apply for Naturalization and How Do I Pay?

The fee for this application is **$330.00**. A **$70.00** biometric services fee for fingerprinting is also required. You should submit both fees with your Form N-400.

For more information on fees and form of payment, call the NCSC at 1-**800-375-5283 (TTY: 1-800-767-1833)** or visit our website at www.uscis.gov and scroll down to Forms and E-Filing."

Your fee is not refundable, even if you withdraw your application or it is denied. If you are unable to pay the naturalization application fee, you may apply in writing for a fee waiver. For information about the fee waiver process, telephone the NCSC at **1-800-375-5283 (TTY: 1-800-767- 1833)** or see the USCIS internet website **(www.uscis.gov)** section "Forms and E-Filing."

## What Do I Send With My Application?

All applicants must send certain documents with their application. For information on the documents and other information you must send with your application, see the Document Checklist in the *Guide.*

## Where Do I Send My Application?

You must send your Form N-400 application and supporting documents to a USCIS Service Center. To find the Service Center address you should use, read the section in the Guide called "Completing Your Application and Getting Photographed" or call the NCSC at **1-800-375-5283 (TTY: 1-800-767-1833).**

Applicants outside the United States who are applying on the basis of their military service should follow the instructions of their designated point of contact at a U.S. military installation.

## How Do I Complete This Application?

- Please print clearly or type your answers using CAPITAL letters in each box.

- Use black ink.

- **Write your USCIS (or former INS) "A"-number on the top right hand corner of each page.** Use your "A"- number on your Permanent Resident Card (formerly known as the Alien Registration or "Green" Card). To locate your "A"- number, see the sample Permanent Resident Cards in the *Guide.* The "A" number on your card consists of seven to nine numbers, depending on when your record was created. If the "A"-number on your card has fewer than nine numbers, place enough zeros before the first number to make a *total of nine numbers* on the application. For example, write card number A1234567 as A001234567, but write card number A12345678 as A012345678.

- If a question does not apply to you, write **N/A** (meaning "Not Applicable") in the space provided.

- If you need extra space to answer any item:
  - -- Attach a separate sheet of paper (or more sheets if needed);
  - -- Write your name, your "A"- number, and "N-400" on the top right corner of the sheet; and
  - -- Write the number of each question for which you are providing additional information.

## Step-by-Step Instructions.

This form is divided into 14 parts. The information below will help you fill out the form.

### Part 1. Your Name *(thePerson Applying for Naturalization).*

**A. Your current legal name** - Your current legal name is the name on your birth certificate, unless it has been changed after birth by a legal action such as a marriage or court order.

**B. Your name exactly as it appears on your Permanent Resident Card** *(if different from above)*-- Write your name exactly as it appears on your card, even if it is misspelled.

**C. Other names you have used** - If you have used any other names in your life, write them in this section. If you need more space, use a separate sheet of paper.

If you have **never** used a different name, write "N/A" in the space for "Family Name *(Last Name)."*

**D. Name change** *(optional)* - A court can allow a change in your name when you are being naturalized. A name change does not become final until a court naturalizes you. For more information regarding a name change, see the *Guide.*

If you want a court to change your name at a naturalization oath ceremony, check "Yes" and complete this section. If you do not want to change your name, check "No" and go to Part 2.

---

**Part 2. Information About Your Eligibility.**

---

Check the box that shows why you are eligible to apply for naturalization. If the basis for your eligibility is not described in one of the first three boxes, check "Other" and briefly write the basis for your application on the lines provided.

---

**Part 3. Information About You.**

---

**A. U.S. Social Security number** - Print your U.S. Social Security number. If you do not have one, write "N/A" in the space provided.

**B. Date of birth** - Always use eight numbers to show your date of birth. Write the date in this order: Month, Day, Year. For example, write May 1, 1958 as 05/01/1958.

**C. Date you became a Permanent Resident** - Write the official date when your lawful permanent residence began, as shown on your Permanent Resident Card. To help locate the date on your card, see the sample Permanent Resident Cards in the *Guide.* Write the date in this order: Month, Day, Year. For example, write August 9, 1988 as 08/09/1988.

**D. Country of birth** - Write the name of the country where you were born. Write the name of the country even if it no longer exists.

**E. Country of nationality** - Write the name of the country where you are currently a citizen or national. Write the name of the country even if it no longer exists.

- If you are stateless, write the name of the country where you were last a citizen or national.

- If you are a citizen or national of more than one country, write the name of the foreign country that issued your last passport.

**F. Citizenship of parents** - Check "Yes" if either of your parents is a U.S. citizen. If you answer "Yes," you may already be a citizen. For more information, see "Frequently Asked Questions" in the *Guide.*

**G. Current marital status** - Check the marital status you have on the date you are filing this application. If you are currently not married, but had a prior marriage that was annulled (declared by a court to be invalid) check "Other" and explain it.

**H. Request for disability waiver** - If you have a medical disability or impairment that you believe qualifies you for a waiver of the tests of English and/or U.S. government and history, check "Yes" and attach a properly completed Form N-648, Medical Certification for Disability Exceptions. If you ask for this waiver it does not guarantee that you will be excused from the testing requirements. For more information about this waiver, see the *Guide.*

**I. Request for disability accommodations** - We will make every reasonable effort to help applicants with disabilities complete the naturalization process. For example, if you use a wheelchair, we will make sure that you can be fingerprinted and interviewed, and can attend a naturalization ceremony at a location that is wheelchair accessible. If you are deaf or hearing impaired and need a sign language interpreter, we will make arrangements with you to have one at your interview.

If you believe you will need us to modify or change the naturalization process for you, check the box or write in the space the kind of accommodation you need. If you need more space, use a separate sheet of paper. You do not need to send us a Form N-648 to request an accommodation. You only need to send a Form N-648 to request a waiver of the test of English and/or civics.

We consider requests for accommodations on a case-by-case basis. Asking for an accommodation will not affect your eligibility for citizenship.

## Part 4. Addresses and Telephone Numbers.

A. **Home address** - Give the address where you now live. Do **not** put post office (P.O.) box numbers here.

B. **Mailing address** - If your mailing address is the same as your home address, write "same." If your mailing address is different from your home address, write it in this part.

C. **Telephone numbers (optional)** - If you give us your telephone numbers and e-mail address, we can contact you about your application more quickly. If you are hearing impaired and use a TTY telephone connection, please indicate this by writing "(TTY)" after the telephone number.

## Part 5. Information for Criminal Records Search.

The Federal Bureau of Investigation (FBI) will use the information in this section, together with your fingerprints, to search for criminal records. Although the results of this search may affect your eligibility, we do **not** make naturalization decisions based on your gender, race or physical description.

For each item, check the box or boxes that best describes you. The categories are those used by the FBI. You can select one or more.

**NOTE:** As part of the USCIS biometric services requirement, you must be fingerprinted after you file this application. If necessary, USCIS may also take your photograph and signature. Check our website at **www.uscis.gov** or call our National Customer Service Center at **1-800-375-5253** to determine the fee for the biometric services.

## Part 6. Information About Your Residence and Employment.

A. Write every address where you have lived during the last five years (including in other countries).

Begin with where you live now. Include the dates you lived in those places. For example, write May 1998 to June 1999 as 05/1998 to 06/1999.

If you need separate sheets of paper to complete section A or B or any other questions on this application, be sure to follow the Instructions in **"How Do I Complete This Application?"** on **Page 2.**

B. List where you have worked (or, if you were a student, the schools you have attended) during the last five years. Include military service. If you worked for yourself, write "self employed." Begin with your most recent job. Also, write the dates when you worked or studied in each place.

## Part 7. Time Outside the United States *(Including Trips to Canada, Mexico and the Caribbean).*

A. Write the total number of days you spent outside of the United States (including on military service) during the last five years. Count the days of every trip that lasted 24 hours or longer.

B. Write the number of trips you have taken outside the United States during the last five years. Count every trip that lasted 24 hours or longer.

C. Provide the requested information for every trip that you have taken outside the United States since you became a Lawful Permanent Resident. Begin with your most recent trip.

## Part 8. Information About Your Marital History.

A. Write the number of times you have been married. Include any annulled marriages. If you were married to the same spouse more than one time, count each time as a separate marriage.

B. If you are now married, provide information about your current spouse.

C. Check the box to indicate whether your current spouse is a U.S. citizen.

**D.** If your spouse is a citizen through naturalization, give the date and place of naturalization. If your spouse regained U.S. citizenship, write the date and place the citizenship was regained.

**E.** If your spouse is not a U.S. citizen, complete this section.

**F.** If you were married before, give information about your former spouse or spouses. In question F.2, check the box showing the immigration status your former spouse had during your marriage. If the spouse was not a U.S. citizen or a Lawful Permanent Resident at that time check "Other" and explain. For question F.5, if your marriage was annulled, check "Other" and explain. If you were married to the same spouse more than one time, write about each marriage separately.

**G.** For any prior marriages of your current spouse, follow the instructions in section F above.

**NOTE:** If you or your present spouse had more than one prior marriage, provide the same information required by section F and section G about every additional marriage on a separate sheet of paper.

### Part 9. Information About Your Children.

**A.** Write the total number of sons and daughters you have had. Count **all** of your children, regardless of whether they are:

- Alive, missing, or dead;
- Born in other countries or in the United States;
- Under 18 years old or adults;
- Married or unmarried;
- Living with you or elsewhere;
- Stepsons or stepdaughters or legally adopted; or

**B.** • Born when you were not married.

Write information about all your sons and daughters. In the last column ("Location"), write:

- "With me" - if the son or daughter is currently living with you;
- The street address and state or country where the son or daughter lives - if the son or daughter is **not** currently living with you; or

- "Missing" or "dead" - if that son or daughter is missing or dead.

If you need space to list information about additional sons and daughters, attach a separate sheet of paper.

### Part 10. Additional Questions.

Answer each question by checking "Yes" or "No." If **any** part of a question applies to you, you must answer "Yes." For example, if you were never arrested but *were* once detained by a police officer, check "Yes" to the question "Have you ever been arrested or detained by a law enforcement officer?" and attach a written explanation.

We will use this information to determine your eligibility for citizenship. Answer every question honestly and accurately. If you do not, we may deny your application for lack of good moral character. Answering "Yes" to one of these questions does not always cause an application to be denied. For more information on eligibility, please see the *Guide*.

### Part 11. Your Signature.

After reading the statement in Part 11, you must sign and date it. You should sign your full name without abbreviating it or using initials. The signature must be legible. Your application may be returned to you if it is not signed.

If you cannot sign your name in English, sign in your native language. If you are unable to write in any language, sign your name with an "X."

**NOTE:** A designated representative may sign this section on behalf an applicant who qualifies for a waiver of the Oath of Allegiance because of a development or physical impairment (see *Guide* for more information). In such a case the designated representative should write the name of the applicant and then sign his or her own name followed by the words "Designated Representative." The information attested to by the Designated Representative is subject to the same penalties discussed on **Page 6** of these Instructions.

## Part 12. Signature of Person Who Prepared the Form for You.

If someone filled out this form for you, he or she must complete this section.

## Part 13. Signature at Interview.

*Do not complete this part. You will be asked to complete this part at your interview.*

## Part 14. Oath of Allegiance.

*Do not complete this part. You will be asked to complete this part at your interview.*

If we approve your application, you must take this Oath of Allegiance to become a citizen. In limited cases you can take a modified Oath. The Oath requirement cannot be waived unless you are unable to understand its meaning because of a physical or developmental disability or mental impairment. For more information, see the *Guide.* Your signature on this form only indicates that you have no objections to taking the Oath of Allegiance. **It does not mean that you have taken the Oath or that you are naturalized**. If USCIS approves your application for naturalization, you must attend an oath ceremony and take the Oath of Allegiance to the United States.

## Penalties.

If you knowingly and willfully falsify or conceal a material fact or submit a false document with this request, we will deny your application for naturalization and may deny any other immigration benefit. In addition, you will face severe penalties provided by law and may be subject to a removal proceeding or criminal prosecution.

If we grant you citizenship after you falsify or conceal a material fact or submit a false document with this request, your naturalization may be revoked.

## Privacy Act Notice.

We ask for the information on this form and for other documents to determine your eligibility for naturalization. Form N-400 processes are generally covered in 8 U.S.C. 1421 through 1430 and 1436 through 1449. We may provide information from your application to other government agencies.

## Use InfoPass for Appointments.

As an alternative to waiting in line for assistance at your local USCIS office, you can now schedule an appointment through our internet-based system, **InfoPass**. To access the system, visit our website at www.uscis.gov. Use the **InfoPass** appointment scheduler and follow the screen prompts to set up your appointment. **InfoPass** generates an electronic appointment notice that appears on the screen. Print the notice and take it with you to your appointment. The notice gives the time and date of your appointment, along with the address of the USCIS office.

## Paperwork Reduction Act Notice.

A person is not required to respond to a collection of information unless it displays a valid OMB control number.

We try to create forms and instructions that are accurate, can be easily understood and that impose the least possible burden on you to provide us with the information. Often this is difficult because some immigration laws are very complex.

The estimated average time to complete and file this form is computed as follows: (1) 2 hours and 8 minutes to learn about and complete the form; (2) 4 hours to assemble and file the information - for a total estimated average of 6 hours and 8 minutes per application.

If you have comments about the accuracy of this estimate or suggestions to make this form simpler, you may write to the U.S. Citizenship and Immigration Services, Regulatory Management Division, 111 Massachusetts Avenue N.W., Washington, DC 20529; OMB No. 1615-0052. **Do not mail your completed application to this address.**

**Department of Homeland Security**
U.S Citizenship and Immigration Services

Print clearly or type your answers using CAPITAL letters. Failure to print clearly may delay your application. Use black ink.

## Part 1. Your Name. *(The Person Applying for Naturalization)*

Write your USCIS "A"- number here:
A

**A**. Your current legal name.

Family Name *(Last Name)*

Given Name *(First Name)*

Full Middle Name *(If applicable)*

**B.** Your name **exactly** as it appears on your Permanent Resident Card.

Family Name *(Last Name)*

Given Name *(First Name)*

Full Middle Name *(If applicable)*

**For USCIS Use Only**

| Bar Code | Date Stamp |
|---|---|
| | Remarks |

**C.** If you have ever used other names, provide them below.

| Family Name *(Last Name)* | Given Name *(First Name)* | Middle Name |
|---|---|---|
| | | |
| | | |

**D.** Name change *(optional)*

Please read the Instructions before you decide whether to change your name.

**1.** Would you like to legally change your name?  ☐ Yes  ☐ No

**2.** If "Yes," print the new name you would like to use. Do not use initials or abbreviations when writing your new name.

Family Name *(Last Name)*

Given Name *(First Name)*

Full Middle Name

Action Block

## Part 2. Information About Your Eligibility. *(Check Only One)*

I am at least 18 years old **AND**

**A.** ☐ I have been a Lawful Permanent Resident of the United States for at least five years.

**B.** ☐ I have been a Lawful Permanent Resident of the United States for at least three years, **and** I have been married to and living with the same U.S. citizen for the last three years, **and** my spouse has been a U.S. citizen for the last three years.

**C.** ☐ I am applying on the basis of qualifying military service.

**D.** ☐ Other *(Please explain)* _____

## Part 3. Information About You.

Write your USCIS "A"- number here:
A

**A.** U.S. Social Security Number

**B.** Date of Birth *(mm/dd/yyyy)*

**C.** Date You Became a Permanent Resident *(mm/dd/yyyy)*

**D.** Country of Birth

**E.** Country of Nationality

**F.** Are either of your parents U.S. citizens? *(if yes, see Instructions)*  ☐ Yes  ☐ No

**G.** What is your current marital status?  ☐ Single, Never Married  ☐ Married  ☐ Divorced  ☐ Widowed

☐ Marriage Annulled or Other *(Explain)* _____

**H.** Are you requesting a waiver of the English and/or U.S. History and Government requirements based on a disability or impairment and attaching a Form N-648 with your application?  ☐ Yes  ☐ No

**I.** Are you requesting an accommodation to the naturalization process because of a disability or impairment? *(See Instructions for some examples of accommodations.)*  Yes ☐

If you answered "Yes," check the box below that applies:

☐ I am deaf or hearing impaired and need a sign language interpreter who uses the following language: _____

☐ I use a wheelchair.

☐ I am blind or sight impaired.

☐ I will need another type of accommodation. Please explain: _____

_____

_____

## Part 4. Addresses and Telephone Numbers.

**A.** Home Address - Street Number and Name *(Do **not** write a P.O. Box in this space)*    Apartment Number

City    County    State    ZIP Code    Country

**B.** Care of    Mailing Address - Street Number and Name *(If different from home address)*    Apartment Number

City    State    ZIP Code    Country

**C.** Daytime Phone Number *(If any)*    Evening Phone Number *(If any)*    E-mail Address *(If any)*

(    )    (    )

Write your  USCIS  "A"- number here:

A

**NOTE:** The categories below are those required by the FBI. See Instructions for more information.

**A.** Gender

☐ Male    ☐ Female

**B.** Height

| Feet | Inches |
|------|--------|

**C.** Weight

| Pounds |
|--------|

**D.** Are you Hispanic or Latino?    ☐ Yes    ☐ No

**E.** Race *(Select one or more.)*

☐ White    ☐ Asian    ☐ Black or African
                                        American    ☐ American Indian or Alaskan Native    ☐ Native Hawaiian or
                                                                                                                                         Other Pacific Islander

**F.** Hair color

☐ Black    ☐ Brown    ☐ Blonde    ☐ Gray    ☐ White    ☐ Red    ☐ Sandy    ☐ Bald (No Hair)

**G.** Eye color

☐ Brown    ☐ Blue    ☐ Green    ☐ Hazel    ☐ Gray    ☐ Black    ☐ Pink    ☐ Maroon    ☐ Other

**Part 6.  Information About Your Residence and Employment.**

**A.**  Where have you lived during the last five years? Begin with where you live now and then every place you lived for the last five
years. If you need more space, use a separate sheet(s) of paper.

| Street Number and Name, Apartment Number, City, State, Zip Code and Country | Dates *(mm/dd/yyyy)* | |
|---|---|---|
| | From | To |
| Current Home Address - Same as Part | | Present |
| | | |
| | | |
| | | |

**B.**  Where have you worked (or, if you were a student, what schools did you attend) during the last five years?  Include military service.
Begin with your current or latest employer and then list every place you have worked or studied for the last five years.  If you need
more space, use a separate sheet of paper.

| Employer or School Name | Employer or School Address *(Street, City and State)* | Dates *(mm/dd/yyyy)* | | Your Occupation |
|---|---|---|---|---|
| | | From | To | |
| | | | | |
| | | | | |
| | | | | |
| | | | | |
| | | | | |

. How many total days did you spend outside of the United States during the past five years? [     ] days

. How many trips of 24 hours or more have you taken outside of the United States during the past five years? [     ] trips

. List below all the trips of 24 hours or more that you have taken outside of the United States since becoming a Lawful Permanent Resident. Begin with your most recent trip. If you need more space, use a separate sheet(s) of paper.

| Date You Left the United States *(mm/dd/yyyy)* | Date You Returned to the United States *(mm/dd/yyyy)* | Did Trip Last Six Months or More? | | Countries to Which You Traveled | Total Days Out of the United States |
|---|---|---|---|---|---|
| | | ☐ Yes | ☐ No | | |
| | | ☐ Yes | ☐ No | | |
| | | ☐ Yes | ☐ No | | |
| | | ☐ Yes | ☐ No | | |
| | | ☐ Yes | ☐ No | | |
| | | ☐ Yes | ☐ No | | |
| | | ☐ Yes | ☐ No | | |
| | | ☐ Yes | | | |

**Part 8.  Information About Your Marital History.**

**A.** How many times have you been married (including annulled marriages)? [     ]  If you have **never** been married, go to Part 9.

**B.** If you are now married, give the following information about your spouse:

**1.** Spouse's Family Name *(Last Name)*          Given Name *(First Name)*          Full Middle Name *(If applicable)*

[                    ]          [                    ]          [                    ]

**2.** Date of Birth  *(mm/dd/yyyy)*          **3.** Date of Marriage *(mm/dd/yyyy)*          **4.** Spouse's U.S. Social Security #

[                    ]          [                    ]          [                    ]

**5.** Home Address - Street Number and Name                              Apartment Number

[                    ]          [                    ]

City                              State                              Zip Code

[                    ]          [                    ]          [                    ]

Write your USCIS "A"- number here:
A

**C.** Is your spouse a U.S. citizen? ☐ Yes ☐ No

**D.** If your spouse is a U.S. citizen, give the following information:

    **1.** When did your spouse become a U.S. citizen? ☐ At Birth ☐ Other

    If "Other," give the following information:

    **2.** Date your spouse became a U.S. citizen

    **3.** Place your spouse became a U.S. citizen *(Please see Instructions)*

    City and State

**E.** If your spouse is **not** a U.S. citizen, give the following information :

    **1.** Spouse's Country of Citizenship

    **2.** Spouse's USCIS "A"- Number *(If applicable)*

    A

    **3.** Spouse's Immigration Status

    ☐ Lawful Permanent Resident ☐ Other _____

**F.** If you were married before, provide the following information about your prior spouse. If you have more than one previous marriage, use a separate sheet(s) of paper to provide the information required in Questions 1-5 below.

    **1.** Prior Spouse's Family Name *(Last Name)*    Given Name *(First Name)*    Full Middle Name *(If applicable)*

    **2.** Prior Spouse's Immigration Status

    ☐ U.S. Citizen

    ☐ Lawful Permanent Resident

    ☐ Other _____

    **3.** Date of Marriage *(mm/dd/yyyy)*

    **4.** Date Marriage Ended *(mm/dd/yyyy)*

    **5.** How Marriage Ended

    ☐ Divorce ☐ Spouse Died ☐ Other _____

**G.** How many times has your current spouse been married (including annulled marriages)? ☐

    If your spouse has **ever** been married before, give the following information about **your spouse's** prior marriage.
    If your spouse has more than one previous marriage, use a separate sheet(s) of paper to provide the information requested in Questions 1 - 5 below.

    **1.** Prior Spouse's Family Name *(Last Name)*    Given Name *(First Name)*    Full Middle Name *(If applicable)*

    **2.** Prior Spouse's Immigration Status

    ☐ U.S. Citizen

    ☐ Lawful Permanent Resident

    ☐ Other _____

    **3.** Date of Marriage *(mm/dd/yyyy)*

    **4.** Date Marriage Ended *(mm/dd/yyyy)*

    **5.** How Marriage Ended

    ☐ Divorce ☐ Spouse Died ☐ Other _____

## Part 9. Information About Your Children.

**A.** How many sons and daughters have you had? For more information on which sons and daughters you should include and how to complete this section, see the Instructions.

**B.** Provide the following information about all of your sons and daughters. If you need more space, use a separate sheet(s) of paper.

| Full Name of Son or Daughter | Date of Birth (mm/dd/yyyy) | USCIS "A"- number (if child has one) | Country of Birth | Current Address (Street, City, State and Country) |
|---|---|---|---|---|
| | | A | | |
| | | A | | |
| | | A | | |
| | | A | | |
| | | A | | |
| | | A | | |
| | | A | | |
| | | A | | |

## Part 10. Additional Questions.

Please answer Questions 1 through 14. If you answer "Yes" to any of these questions, include a written explanation with this form. Your written explanation should (1) explain why your answer was "Yes" and (2) provide any additional information that helps to explain your answer.

### A. General Questions.

1. Have you **ever** claimed to be a U.S. citizen *(in writing or any other way)*?  ☐ Yes  ☐ No

2. Have you **ever** registered to vote in any Federal, state or local election in the United States?  ☐ Yes  ☐ No

3. Have you **ever** voted in any Federal, state or local election in the United States?  ☐ Yes  ☐ No

4. Since becoming a Lawful Permanent Resident, have you **ever** failed to file a required Federal, state or local tax return?  ☐ Yes  ☐ No

5. Do you owe any Federal, state or local taxes that are overdue?  ☐ Yes  ☐ No

6. Do you have any title of nobility in any foreign country?  ☐ Yes  ☐ No

7. Have you ever been declared legally incompetent or been confined to a mental institution within the last five years?  ☐ Yes  ☐ No

### B. Affiliations.

8.  **a.** Have you **ever** been a member of or associated with any organization, association, fund, foundation, party, club, society or similar group in the United States or in any other place?   ☐ Yes   ☐ No

    **b.** If you answered "Yes," list the name of each group below. If you need more space, attach the names of the other group(s) on a separate sheet(s) of paper.

| Name of Group | Name of Group |
|---|---|
| 1. | 6. |
| 2. | 7. |
| 3. | 8. |
| 4. | 9. |
| 5. | 10. |

9.  Have you **ever** been a member of or in any way associated *(either directly or indirectly)* with:

    **a.** The Communist Party?   ☐ Yes   ☐ No

    **b.** Any other totalitarian party?   ☐ Yes   ☐ No

    **c.** A terrorist organization?   ☐ Yes   ☐ No

10. Have you **ever** advocated *(either directly or indirectly)* the overthrow of any government by force or violence?   ☐ Yes   ☐ No

11. Have you **ever** persecuted *(either directly or indirectly)* any person because of race, religion, national origin, membership in a particular social group or political opinion?   ☐ Yes   ☐ No

12. Between March 23, 1933 and May 8, 1945, did you work for or associate in any way *(either directly or indirectly)* with:

    **a.** The Nazi government of Germany?   ☐ Yes   ☐ No

    **b.** Any government in any area (1) occupied by, (2) allied with, or (3) established with the help of the Nazi government of Germany?   ☐ Yes   ☐ No

    **c.** Any German, Nazi, or S.S. military unit, paramilitary unit, self-defense unit, vigilante unit, citizen unit, police unit, government agency or office, extermination camp, concentration camp, prisoner of war camp, prison, labor camp or transit camp?   ☐ Yes   ☐ No

### C. Continuous Residence.

Since becoming a Lawful Permanent Resident of the United States:

13. Have you **ever** called yourself a "nonresident" on a Federal, state or local tax return?   ☐ Yes   ☐ No

14. Have you **ever** failed to file a Federal, state or local tax return because you considered yourself to be a "nonresident"?   ☐ Yes   ☐ No

Write your USCIS "A"- number here:
A

**D. Good Moral Character.**

For the purposes of this application, you must answer "Yes" to the following questions, if applicable, even if your records were sealed or otherwise cleared or if anyone, including a judge, law enforcement officer or attorney, told you that you no longer have a record.

15. Have you **ever** committed a crime or offense for which you were **not** arrested? ☐ Yes ☐ No

16. Have you **ever** been arrested, cited or detained by any law enforcement officer (including USCIS or former INS and military officers) for any reason? ☐ Yes ☐ No

17. Have you **ever** been charged with committing any crime or offense? ☐ Yes ☐ No

18. Have you **ever** been convicted of a crime or offense? ☐ Yes ☐ No

19. Have you **ever** been placed in an alternative sentencing or a rehabilitative program (for example: diversion, deferred prosecution, withheld adjudication, deferred adjudication)? ☐ Yes ☐ No

20. Have you **ever** received a suspended sentence, been placed on probation or been paroled? ☐ ☐ No

21. Have you **ever** been in jail or prison? ☐ No

If you answered "Yes" to any of Questions 15 through 21, complete the following ) If y ed more spa a separate sheet (s) of paper to give the same information.

| Why were you arrested, cited, detained or charged? | te arreste ined or ge /dd/yy | A M were rrested, cit etained or charged? (City, State, Country) | Outcome or disposition of the arrest, citation, detention or charge *(No charges filed, charges dismissed, jail, probation, etc.)* |
|---|---|---|---|
| | | | |
| | | | |
| | | | |

Answer Questions 22 through 33. If you answer "Yes" to any of these questions, attach (1) your written explanation why your answer was "Yes" and (2) any additional information or documentation that helps explain your answer.

22. Have you **ever**:

    **a.** Been a habitual drunkard? ☐ Yes ☐ No

    **b.** Been a prostitute, or procured anyone for prostitution? ☐ Yes ☐ No

    **c.** Sold or smuggled controlled substances, illegal drugs or narcotics? ☐ Yes ☐ No

    **d.** Been married to more than one person at the same time? ☐ Yes ☐ No

    **e.** Helped anyone enter or try to enter the United States illegally? ☐ Yes ☐ No

    **f.** Gambled illegally or received income from illegal gambling? ☐ Yes ☐ No

    **g.** Failed to support your dependents or to pay alimony? ☐ Yes ☐ No

23. Have you **ever** given false or misleading information to any U.S. government official while applying for any immigration benefit or to prevent deportation, exclusion or removal? ☐ Yes ☐ No

24. Have you **ever** lied to any U.S. government official to gain entry or admission into the United States? ☐ Yes ☐ No

### E. Removal, Exclusion and Deportation Proceedings.

25. Are removal, exclusion, rescission or deportation proceedings pending against you? ☐ Yes ☐ No

26. Have you **ever** been removed, excluded or deported from the United States? ☐ Yes ☐ No

27. Have you **ever** been ordered to be removed, excluded or deported from the United States? ☐ Yes ☐ No

28. Have you **ever** applied for any kind of relief from removal, exclusion or deportation? ☐ Yes ☐ No

### F. Military Service.

29. Have you **ever** served in the U.S. Armed Forces? ☐ Yes ☐ No

30. Have you **ever** left the United States to avoid being drafted into the U.S. Armed Forces? ☐ Yes ☐ No

31. Have you **ever** applied for any kind of exemption from military service in the U.S. Armed Forces? ☐ Yes ☐ No

32. Have you **ever** deserted from the U.S. Armed Forces? ☐ Yes ☐ No

### G. Selective Service Registration.

33. Are you a male who lived in the United States at any time between your 18th and 26th birthdays in any status except as a lawful nonimmigrant? ☐ Yes ☐ No

If you answered "NO," go on to question 34.

If you answered "YES," provide the information below.

If you answered "YES," but you did not register with the Selective Service System and are still under 26 years of age, you must register before you apply for naturalization, so that you can complete the information below:

| Date Registered (mm/dd/yyyy) | | Selective Service Number | |
| --- | --- | --- | --- |

If you answered "YES," but you did not register with the Selective Service and you are now 26 years old or older, attach a statement explaining why you did not register.

### H. Oath Requirements. *(See Part 14 for the Text of the Oath)*

Answer Questions 34 through 39. If you answer "No" to any of these questions, attach (1) your written explanation why the answer was "No" and (2) any additional information or documentation that helps to explain your answer.

34. Do you support the Constitution and form of government of the United States? ☐ Yes ☐ No

35. Do you understand the full Oath of Allegiance to the United States? ☐ Yes ☐ No

36. Are you willing to take the full Oath of Allegiance to the United States? ☐ Yes ☐ No

37. If the law requires it, are you willing to bear arms on behalf of the United States? ☐ Yes ☐ No

38. If the law requires it, are you willing to perform noncombatant services in the U.S. Armed Forces? ☐ Yes ☐ No

39. If the law requires it, are you willing to perform work of national importance under civilian direction? ☐ Yes ☐ No

## Part 11. Your Signature.

Write your USCIS "A"- number here:
A

I certify, under penalty of perjury under the laws of the United States of America, that this application, and the evidence submitted with it, are all true and correct. I authorize the release of any information that the USCIS needs to determine my eligibility for naturalization.

Your Signature

Date (mm/dd/yyyy)

## Part 12. Signature of Person Who Prepared This Application for You. *(If Applicable)*

I declare under penalty of perjury that I prepared this application at the request of the above person. The answers provided are based on information of which I have personal knowledge and/or were provided to me by the above named person in response to the *exact questions* contained on this form.

Preparer's Printed Name

Preparer's Signaure

Date (mm/dd/yyyy)

Preparer's Firm or Organization Name (If applicable)

Preparer's Daytime Phone Number

Preparer's Address - Street Number and Name

City

State

Zip Code

**NOTE: Do not complete Parts 13 a~~nd~~ ~~un~~ ~~til~~ ~~a USCIS o~~fficer instructs you to do so.**

## Part 13. Signature at Interview

I swear (affirm) and certify under penalty of perjury under the laws of the United States of America that I know that the contents of this application for naturalization subscribed by me, including corrections numbered 1 through _____ and the evidence submitted by me numbered pages 1 through _____ , are true and correct to the best of my knowledge and belief.

Subscribed to and sworn to (affirmed) before me

Officer's Printed Name or Stamp

Date (mm/dd/yyyy)

Complete Signature of Applicant

Officer's Signature

## Part 14. Oath of Allegiance.

If your application is approved, you will be scheduled for a public oath ceremony at which time you will be required to take the following oath of allegiance immediately prior to becoming a naturalized citizen. By signing, you acknowledge your willingness and ability to take this oath:

I hereby declare, on oath, that I absolutely and entirely renounce and abjure all allegiance and fidelity to any foreign prince, potentate, state, or sovereignty, of whom or which which I have heretofore been a subject or citizen;

that I will support and defend the Constitution and laws of the United States of America against all enemies, foreign and domestic;

that I will bear true faith and allegiance to the same;

that I will bear arms on behalf of the United States when required by the law;

that I will perform noncombatant service in the Armed Forces of the United States when required by the law;

that I will perform work of national importance under civilian direction when required by the law; and

that I take this obligation freely, without any mental reservation or purpose of evasion; so help me God.

Printed Name of Applicant

Complete Signature of Applicant

# USCIS Is Making Photos Simpler

**Old Three-Quarter Style Photo**

**New Passport Style Photo**

**Photos Must Be in Color**

**Washington, DC** — In accordance with language specified in the Border Security Act of 2003, U.S. Citizenship and Immigration Services (USCIS) announced a change in the photo requirements for all applicants from a three-quarter face position to a standard, full-frontal face position to take effect **August 2, 2004**.

USCIS will accept both three-quarter and full-frontal color photographs until **September 1, 2004,** after which only full-frontal color will be accepted.

The application process of customers who have already submitted materials that include color photos with the three-quarter standard **will not** be affected by this change.

All photos must be of just the person. Where more than one photo is required, all photos of the person must be identical. All photos must meet the specifications for full-frontal/passport photos.

For more information on photo standards, visit the Department of State website at http://www.travel.state.gov/passport/pptphotos/index.html, or contact the USCIS National Customer Service Center at 1 800 375 5283.

List of forms that require photos is on the back

## 2 photos are required for the following forms:

**I-90** – Renew or replace your Permanent Resident Card (green card)

**I-131** – Re-entry permit, refugee travel document, or advance parole

**I-485** – Adjust status and become a permanent resident while in the U.S.

**I-765** – Employment Authorization/Employment Authorization Document (EAD)

**I-777** – Replace Northern Mariana Card

**I-821** – Temporary Protected Status (TPS) Program

**N-300** – Declaration of Intent (to apply for U.S. citizenship)

**N-400** – Naturalization (to become a U.S. citizen)

**N-565** – Replace Naturalization/Citizenship Certificate

## 3 photos are required for the following forms:

**I-698** – Temporary Resident's application under the 1987 Legalization Program for permanent resident status — file 1 photo for your application, and bring the other 2 with you to your interview

**N-600K** – To apply for U.S. citizenship for foreign-born child residing abroad with U.S. citizen parent

## 4 photos are required for the following forms:

**I-817** – To apply for Family Unity Benefits

**I-881** – NACARA — suspension of deportation or special rule cancellation

## File the following with your photos and of others as shown below:

**I-129F** – Fiancé(e) Petition — file with 1 photo of you + 1 photo of fiancé(e)

**I-130** – Relative petition — if filing for your husband or wife, file with 1 photo of you + 1 photo of your husband or wife

**I-589** – Asylum — file with 1 photo of you + 1 photo of each family member listed in Part A. II that you are including in your application

**I-730** – Relative petition filed by a person granted Asylum or Refugee status — file with 1 photo of the family member for whom you are filing the I-730

**I-914** – 'T' nonimmigrant status — file with 3 photos of you + 3 photos of each immediate family member for which you file an I-914A supplement

*All photos must be of just the person. Where more than one photo is required, all photos of the person must be identical. All photos must meet the specifications for full-frontal/passport photos.*

For more information, visit our website at www.uscis.gov, or call our customer service at 1 800 375 5283.

# 18 USCIS Office Addresses

**All naturalization applications must be filed at the Regional Service Center that has jurisdiction over your place of residence:**

**Vermont Service Center**
U.S. Department of Homeland Security
USCIS
Attn: N-400 Unit
75 Lower Welden Street
St. Albans, VT 05479-0001

*This office has jurisdiction over the following states:*
MA, CT, NH, RI, NY, PA, DE, WV, MD, NJ, DC, VA, ME, VT and also has jurisdiction over the INS offices in: Puerto Rico, Bermuda, Toronto, Montreal, Virgin Islands and Dominican Republic


**Nebraska Service Center**
USCIS
Attn: N-400 Unit
PO Box 87400
Lincoln, NE 68501-7400

*This office has jurisdiction over the following states:*
MI, IL, IN, WI, OR, AK, MN, ND, SD, KS, MO, WA, ID, CO, UT, WY, OH, NE, IA, and also has jurisdiction over the following INS offices: Manitoba, British Columbia and Calgary

**Texas Service Center**
USCIS
Attn: N-400 Unit
PO Box 851204
Mesquite, TX 75185-1204

*This office has jurisdiction over the following states:*
FL, TX, NM, OK, GA, NC, SC, AL, LA, AR, MS, TN, KY, and also has jurisdic-tion over the following INS offices: Bahamas, Freeport and Nassau

**California Service Center**
USCIS
Attn: N-400 Unit
P.O. Box 10400
Laguna Niguel, CA 92607-1040

*This office has jurisdiction over the following states:*
CA, HI, AZ, NV and Guam

# 19 U.S. Passport Agencies

**These offices serve customers who are traveling within 2 weeks (14 days), or who need foreign visas to travel.**

**Most offices open between 8:00 and 9:00 a.m. and close between 3:00 and 4:00 p.m., Monday through Friday, excluding Federal holidays**

### Boston, Massachusetts
Thomas P. O'Neill Federal Building
10 Causeway Street, Suite 247
Boston, MA 02222-1094
Automated Appointment Number: (877) 487-2778

### Chicago, Illinois
Kluczynski Federal Office Building
230 S. Dearborn, 18th Floor
Chicago, IL 60604-1564
Automated Appointment Number: (312) 341-6020

### Honolulu, Hawaii
Prince Kuhio Federal Building
300 Ala Moana Blvd.-Suite 1-330
Honolulu, HI 96850
Recorded Information: (808) 522-8283

### Houston, Texas
Mickey Leland Federal Building
1919 Smith Street, Suite 1400
Houston, TX 77002-8049
Automated Appointment Number: (713) 751-0294

## Norwalk, Connecticut
50 Washington Street
Norwalk, CT 06854
Automated Appointment Number: (203) 299-5443

## Los Angeles, California
Federal Building
11000 Wilshire Blvd.-Suite 1000
Los Angeles, CA 90024-3615
Automated Appointment Number: (310) 575-5700

## Miami, Florida
Claude Pepper Federal Office Building
51 SW First Ave.-3rd Floor
Miami, FL 33130-1680
Automated Appointment Number: (305) 539-3600

## New Orleans, Louisiana
One Canal Place (corner of Canal and North Peters Street)
365 Canal Street, Suite 1300
New Orleans, LA 70130-6508
Automated Appointment Number: (504) 412-2600

## New York City, New York
376 Hudson Street
New York, NY 10014
Automated Appointment Number: (212) 206-3500
*Note: This office is no longer able to accept walk-in customers who do not have an appointment.*

## Philadelphia, Pennsylvania
U.S. Custom House
200 Chestnut Street, Room 103
Philadelphia, PA 19106-2970
Automated Appointment Number: (215) 418-5937

**San Francisco, California**
95 Hawthorne Street, 5th Floor
San Francisco, CA 94105-3901
Automated Appointment Number: (415) 538-2700


**Seattle, Washington**
Henry Jackson Federal Building
915 Second Ave.-Suite 992
Seattle, WA 98174-1091
Automated Appointment Number: (206) 808-5700


**Washington, DC**
1111 19th Street, N.W.
Washington, DC 20524
Automated Appointment Number: (202) 647-0518


**Special Issuance Agency**
1111 19th Street, NW, Suite 200
Washington, DC 20036
*Note: Applications for Diplomatic, Official, and No-Fee Passports*

# Index

## W

# BOOK ORDER FORM

Two easy ordering methods:

**Credit Card Orders**
Call the publisher, Next Decade, Inc.
Telephone: 800-595-5440

**Check or Money Orders**
Complete this form, attach your payment,
and mail to:
Next Decade, Inc.
39 Old Farmstead Road, Chester, NJ 07930

If you have any questions, call us:  Telephone: 908-879-6625
Email: info@nextdecade.com    www.nextdecade.com

YOUR NAME AND TITLE: _____

NAME OF ORGANIZATION (if applicable): _____

STREET ADDRESS: _____

CITY: _____ STATE: _____ ZIP: _____

TELEPHONE: _____ FAX: _____

E-MAIL: _____

    Please ship _____ copies of *Citizenship Made Simple* at $16.95 per copy     $ _____

    Please ship _____ copies of *Immigration Made Simple* at $22.95 per copy     $ _____

    NJ orders ONLY add 6% sales tax if required     $ _____

    Shipping: Add $5.00 for the first copy and $1.00 for each additional copy     $ _____

    **I HAVE ENCLOSED THE TOTAL**     $ _____

A check/money order made payable to **Next Decade, Inc.** for $ _____ is enclosed.

Credit Card Payments:    ❑ Visa  ❑ Mastercard

Credit Card # (16 digits) _____ Expiration Date: _____

Name as it appears on the card: _____

Signature: _____